# THE

# PSIONS'

# GUIDE

by
Dr. John Porter, Ph.D., M. Ed.

Coauthored by
Rob Williams, Soke of Hoshin Budo Ryu

Other Books offered by Hoshin Budo Ryu (HBR)

*Hoshin Healing Manual*
*Mandala Therapy*
*Hoshin Games*
*The Unabridged Dictionary of Mysticism, Spiritualism, and the Supernatural*
*Compilation of Hoshin E-mails* (The best questions and answers from members since 1997 to present)
*Hoshin Dim Mak* (Fire belts and up)

*The Psions' Guide*

Published by
Hoshin Budo Ryu
www.hoshin.us

Original cover design by Dr. John Porter
Typeset by Jared Guinn

ISBN 978-0-6151-8588-0

# CONTENTS

# About the Authors

**John Porter** has studied martial arts his entire life, over the past three decades focusing *on Ninpo Ninjutsu* (4<sup>th</sup> dan) and *Hoshin (6<sup>th</sup> dan)*. Dr. Porter has mastered the use of psi skills and has used them extensively to achieve success in his life's pursuits. Dr. Porter has a *Bachelor's degree in Eastern Philosophy*, a *Masters in Physical Education*, a *Masters in Special Education*, and *a Doctorate in Behavioral Psychology*. Through the implementation of the concepts of *Mandala Therapy* and *Psionics*, Dr. Porter has achieved *State Championships in Basketball and Track and Field*, both as a player and as a coach, qualified for the 1980 U.S. Olympic Trials in the Decathlon with a world class score of 7658, and participated in *Cross-Country Horseback Riding* and the *Modern Pentathlon*. He is a licensed *Sailing Captain*. He has been named to the *Who's Who in Business, Who's Who in Martial Arts*, and as an *Outstanding Young American*, and served on the *Ohio Small Business Development Counci*l.

**Rob Williams** has been involved in martial arts training since 1980 and has studied *Jow Ga Kempo, Aikido, Bujinkan Ninpo, Hoshinjutsu, Russian Systema* and several styles of *Kung-fu.* Rob has been a *professional massage, bodywork and energy healing instructor* since 2000. He is an elect member of the *Martial Arts Masters World Federation Sokeship Council.* Rob holds master level rank in all areas of Hoshin combat and esoteric training under Soke Glenn Morris. Rob is a *Hoshin Tao Chi Kung* master and was personally trained and certified by Soke Morris to teach and award rank in Hoshin Tao Chi Kung. Rob went through the *full kundalini awakening* in 1999 under the personal guidance of Soke Morris. He has taught and lectured with Dr. Morris on the subjects of kundalini awakening, energy healing, martial arts, ninpo and chi kung. Rob Williams is the *grandmaster of the Hoshin Budo Ryu.*

## Chapter One

# INTRODUCTION TO PSIONIC ARTS

**P**si is the twenty-third letter of the Greek alphabet. The word is commonly used in parapsychology to include both phenomena of ESP and PK because both are closely related. However, the word is often used inaccurately to include almost any paranormal experience or phenomenon. Psionics is formally known as applied "para-psychology." In the broadest sense, whenever anyone acts on "intuition" or a "hunch", they are using applied parapsychology.

The term "psychic" is from the root word "psyche" meaning "of the soul." In psychic terms it is used to identify phenomena and individuals whose nature is beyond the current bounds of scientific explanation. "Psionics" is the action, or process, of something currently beyond precise, scientific, quantitative, explanation.

Psionics is not a type of magic. Magic is based on the principal that, through the use of words, gestures, and catalyzing materials of unique power, external energies can be controlled. The key element of magic is external energy. The essence of psionic ability is the understanding and mastery of the individual self. Psionics is internal, a creation in the mind. Although psionic powers are centered in the mind, acquiring and controlling these powers demands physical fitness.

Psions are not particularly concerned with the true value of scientific, religious, or pseudoscientific theories about the nature of psychic functioning. They are concerned with the practical utility of such theories for their own use. They are concerned with reliability, consistency, and the magnitude of psi effects, as it appears in the world of business and personal affairs, not in the laboratory.

Psions are unique in that they are self-contained. They do not need any physical weapons, tools, plants, herbs, candles, or deities. The Psion strives to unite every aspect of his/her self into a single, powerful whole. This type of knowledge comes from long and intense directed meditations coupled with physical extremes. The Psion finds enlightenment in both complete exhaustion and complete relaxation, in both pain and pleasure. The Psion carries his/her abilities at all times.

The one way that psi energy has been quantitatively identified is through the measurement of the involuntary physiological processes in the autonomic nervous system of laboratory test subjects. The most common measures are the galvanic skin response (GSR), which records the activity of the sweat gland, and the plethysmorgraph, which measures the changes in blood volume in the finger that are caused by the dilation and constriction of blood vessels. Another method is the electroencephalograph (EEG), which measures brain activity. Psionics then is the effecting of something through the electro-magnetic field, using intention, along with focusing tools and mudras.

The GSR and plethysmorgraph are used to detect emotional arousal. Their use in psi tests indicate when the subject is confronted with emotionally charged targets as opposed to emotionally neutral targets.

Studies with the Ganzfield stimulation show that an alpha state brain-wave appears to be conductive to psi. Psi performance improves with a positive mood and successful expectation is provided by the experimenter while in a friendly atmosphere. Psi decreases when the experimenter sets up conditions for anxiety, a negative mood, expectation, boredom, and a hostile environment.

Theories concerning the function of Psi are difficult to formulate. It defies most laboratory experiments to describe its activity in the physical or quasi-physical terms. Psionic energy is not a physical substance. It is ethereal spirit which prevails all things, and moves the mass of the universe. It is not enclosed in man but radiates within and around us like a luminous sphere. It can be made to act at long distances. It can poison the essence of life and cause disease, or it may purify life and restore health. Through psionics, the existing state of an object or system can be perceived.

The main reason for the failure of modern medicine is that it is dealing with the results of the disorder and not the cause. It's not enough to recognize your physical symptoms, you have to get to know yourself.

Sister M. Smith, Rosary Hill College, Buffalo, NY, 1970, research had focuses on enzymes, large protein molecules, which act as catalysts, speeding up biochemical reactions such as those associated with growth of tissue and wound healing. Her research had shown that the reactivity of enzymes, which were treated by a strong magnetic field, was increased.

Robert Mihalsky and E. Douglas Dean looked at company presidents who had doubled their company's profits during the last five years. They found these individuals scored much higher in the precognitive tests than other executives. The practical applications of a discipline always precede the science and scholarship data. Certainly the same holds true for psi research.

Many people are uncomfortable with the idea their attitudes and emotions create their health problems. It makes them feel as if their illness and misfortunes are their fault. Physicians have long found that when emotional and psychological stress is stabilized, functional and mental disorders, which have strong emotional and psychological components as their underlying causes, often resolve themselves, or can be treated easily. Now that studies have shown a direct connection between emotional stress and heart disease, people are beginning to recognize and respect the link between body and mind.

There are two primary types of psionic techniques, asymmetric and bio-energetic. Asymmetric techniques include exploration, discovery, resolution, and reinforcement of self-regulation processes which relate to specific manifestations of adoption. Bio-energetic techniques act in relation to sets of general correspondences and regulatory functions which exist in the normal healthy body.

All complex systems rely on shared information. The acquisition, management, and response to this information is ongoing and occurs continuously in the moment. This dynamic process is commonly referred to as "self-regulation". Functional dynamics, the principles that techniques are built on, are the recognition of relationships, correspondences, actions and reactions. Functional dynamics guide the technical process. Functional dynamics is the way things work without attention or reliance on how they work. The how they work involves the "mechanisms of action".

## Examples of "mechanisms of action"

- Electro-dynamic fields
- DC current
- Fluid ionic current system
- Various currents associated with embryological development
- Battery properties of the epidermis
- Electrical fields associated with neural and muscular activities
- Sonic, acoustical, phonon properties created by muscle contractions
- Sensitivity of the body to extremely weak electrical fields
- Frequency-dependent correlation between organs
- Electromagnetic properties of acupuncture meridians
- Superconductivity properties of specific tissues & cell structures
- Biophotonic dynamics of living organisms
- Magnetic emanations of organs such as the heart and the brain
- Geophysical/biological field interactions
- Pranic system
- Qi dynamics
- Yogic principles

## Psionic Element

Water is the element of psionic forces. Water can greatly assist or detract from psionic skills, depending on the type of the skill attempted.

## Limitations to Psionic Powers

Psionic powers have definite limitations. Psions have a finite amount of psionic strength available to them at any given time. The Psion must always balance the use of energy for attacks and defenses with other body energy levels and general health. Through the use of meditation a Psion can easily restore psi energy.

Some psionic powers have a range requiring touch. Some require the target mind to be receptive. The human body transfers a tremendous amount of energy. Just as "reflexology", through hand and foot stimulation, energy can influence body systems, these body systems send data back to the hands. Hand-to-hand psionic contact is like plugging in an extension cord. This is one reason we hold hands during courtship, romantic and compatibility information is transferred between bodies.

Some psionic powers require line-of-sight to use. If the line-of-sight is blocked, these psionic techniques will not work. An "obstruction" is anything that hinders a person's normal vision or blocks the line of sight. Even so, a master Psion can often produce techniques to go around obstacles.

**Psionics and Magic**

Psionics and magic use different sources, although their methods may appear to be similar. Psionics uses internal energy, while magic uses external energy. Both arts can produce similar effects. Both use focused intention. Psions use fewer mantras and chants, but more mudras and hand postures.

The Psion works to develop the mind, body, and spirit into a unified, powerful whole. The psionic strength (energy) comes from deep within the self. It is a combination of diet, exercise, mediation, and rest. This energy is given form and purpose by the individual's strength of will. Through extraordinary discipline, meditation, and deepening awareness of self, the Psion taps the vast potential of the mind.

**Alignment**

Psions can not be chaotic. Chaotic people can not maintain the discipline integral to perfecting psionics. When a Psion's alignment shifts to chaotic for any reason, they quickly begin to lose psionic powers. This is because psionic strength is partially increased through the practice; repetitive, consistent, practice, and discipline. Discipline arises from intelligence and wisdom. A person who can make up their mind, take a position, stand for something, and have passion to practice to do something, will make a good Psion. This is the reason why the archetype Psion is often rare and is a solitary figure, they are not crowd followers.

Because the pursuit of psionics requires strict mental and physical discipline, a Psion has three prime requirements; wisdom, constitution, and intelligence. The primary mental ability is wisdom. As the measure of insight and enlightenment, wisdom promotes the understanding and mastery of the inner self, the essence of psionic ability. Likewise, the stress of using psionics requires a healthy body, both physically and mentally. This is where constitution comes into play. Third, intelligence is important to Psions because of the reasoning, focus, and understanding of cause and effect.

## Weapons

Psions are not typically attached to traditional weapons. They understand that the mind is mightier than the sword. The understanding is that guns don't kill, rather the mind that controls the mind that controls the gun kills. Psionic abilities are most effective when applied with stealth. However, when a Psion is dually trained in a martial art, they can often infuse, and hide, the psi powers in their weapons, or through the physical movements, such as in the use of "Dim Mak".

## Defending Yourself from Psionic Attacks

Defenses against psionic attacks include stopping all contact with the suspected people, places, or path of studies; avoid going to the sea, lake, or river; crossing a river and moving on; keep the stomach full. This shuts down the psychic centers which serve as ports of entry; get plenty of sunshine. Sunshine increases brain chemicals which slow psionic influences. It is recommended to sit in a shady area, to avoid damage by direct sunlight, where plenty of sunshine is visible. It is important to take in the sunlight through the optic nerve; avoid being alone. Other people may deflect the energy of an attack, help defend, or help you get to a safe location; and finally, for those with advanced training in magic or psionics, undertake certain protective and banishing rituals.

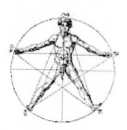

## What Can We Do With Psionics?

There is a lot that can be done with Psionics, regular kinds of everyday things. It really depends on the path it is directed and how it manifests. Psionics has vast potential... all it needs is to manifest, by thought or action and it can create ANYTHING!

Telekinesis, Psycho Kinetics, usually refer to it as *power*. It really isn't a power. Power, usually, denotes a more ego base ideology or reference. I think, "ability" is a more apropos way to refer to it. It is ability. It's the imbalance and misuse, as with many things, that lends fame and glory its disruptive chaos.

## Chapter Two

# EVERYONE HAS THE POTENTIAL

Everyone has the potential to be able to be telekinetic.

There are different things that can have a sort of psychotropic affect on the brain. Meaning; affecting the mental activity, behavior perception. Even stress and abuse can cause one to cultivate certain psychokinetic abilities. I am referring here to the actual ability, not certain mental illness that can mimic telepathy and such. Sometimes, "hearing voices", or "visions" can be the result of very serious emotional, mental illness or organic disturbances. If you think you are having any problems with anything of that nature, please see your doctor.

The brain is the hardware that is utilized by the Mind. Our brain is capable of generating a neural network that when "pushed" can step up to an energy ready state to be utilized beyond our five senses. Neurons do communicate with each other. There are low level subatomic and atomic dialogues going on all the time. Even at a cellular level there is communication going on.

**Psionic Energy is Natural**

These abilities are very natural. Not "freak" happenings or mutant manifestations unnatural to human development. This is a Mind/Brain/Consciousness related phenomenon, though certainly its roots are sub-atomic, like all manifestations. Some research shows there is a lot of activity in the cortex of the brain. Most of what we term psychic phenomenon or mystical happening happens in the "off" phases of consciousness. Consciousness is always in the on/off phasing, blinking off and on, as it where. Off/On phasing phenomenon is photon related… manifestation of energy and light. The energy we are dealing with here is tiny pockets or "quanta" of energies. The ability to bend spoons/ levitate is happening at the other levels being only manifested as a physical event upon the space/time shell frame-which we interpret as our reality. There is also a good deal of illusion as well. One must be able to discern the reality of both. Sometimes, there is a vast difference in what we THINK we see vs. what IS actually happening.

Theoretical Physics can prove this… but then again, theoretical physics can prove that an elephant can hang off a cliff from a flower by its tail so where does that help us as proof? Many things we classify as impossible or not possible *are* real and *are* possible! It's just that either we don't understand the true nature of the event or we as yet have not come to that level of awareness to know what is possible as a natural event. Look at the bumblebee. Theoretically, it shouldn't be able to fly according to our known sciences. Yet, despite their size vs. wing span and weight, they fly!

Many things are possible and do happen. Why do things happen for some and not others? Psionic activity is very much a part of human experience as swimming. Anyone can learn to swim and anyone can learn to cultivate their telekinetic abilities. Keyword, *learn*. It just takes exposure to it and lots, and lots, of practice. Are you born knowing how to play golf? No, of course not, but if many people in your family play golf, you do have the exposure to it and the opportunity. That's 2/3 the equation... the rest as any golfer knows is *practice*!

Some individuals are born with this ability more easily accessible. It is present and already working. They just spend time honing their skills. It works for them without much prompting. For those who have yet to be able to do this or those of you who want to do this we will create a guide for you to follow. Perhaps, it will help you activate your own psionic abilities.

Before you learn what you can do, you should take the time to learn what **NOT to do!**

**What not to do**

Before you get started trying to bend the spoons and forks, let us give you some tips on why it may not work or hasn't been working.

1. The reasons why someone has difficulty cultivating their psionic skills is usually one of several things. Some human emotions like stress can impede the process, though once in awhile a stressful situation can actually increase someone's ability to achieve what appear as supernatural traits. I'm sure you've heard of the situations where all of a sudden something happens and someone can lift a ton of car off someone. Yes, that has to do with adrenaline but there is also a dynamics of "quanta" going on there. In the moment of "have to" they released their natural ability to, seemingly, defy science. They didn't think about it-they just did it. No thinking, no preconceived judgments. Don't think about it so much... just practice without preconceiving.

2. Usually, though, if there isn't any real danger or need, the human emotions inhibit the path that the brain requires to create the neural network it needs to create this atmosphere. The more negative emotions, like guilt, fear, non-trusting, judgmental attitudes and suspicions are enough to inhibit that natural flow that is required. One must believe it is possible. How else can we expect to manifest anything if we can't believe it's possible? You can't.

3. Don't obsess on it – relax!! Enjoy cultivating another skill. It's not a race or test. It's not about worth or worthy. So many spiritually based philosophies are based on reward. Spiritual awareness and evolution are not "prizes" you win. Opening up to higher levels of spiritual awareness is a growth process of evolving one's consciousness. Psionics is just one more skill with the ability of possible manifestation.

4. Don't carry preconceived ideas as to the outcome. Experience it, naturally. Don't script it. Don't tell yourself how it

should go or that you have to be at a certain point at a certain time – all that impedes the energy. When you do that you are so busy thinking that the correct atmosphere or pathway cannot be presented. Will and Reason are not juxtaposed to psionic ability.

5. Don't get frustrated and angry with yourself. Again, relax, Have fun with it.

6. Don't be self-conscious. Many times people feel foolish or self-conscious. Don't. If you can't do it right away it says nothing about who you are. It simply just says the spoon or fork isn't bending, yet – that's all.

## What can we do?

1. What we can do is have an accepting attitude. Believe it can happen. Anyone who ever taught psi and who was successful in bending a fork or spoon had a POSITIVE attitude about it. They may not have believed they could do it but they did believe it was possible. That's a start for the proper frame of mind. Next, believe YOU can!!

2. Focus your attention. So many people say they are concentrating but in fact their minds are scattered and they aren't really into it at all. Be there. Learn to do only one thing at a time. This is difficult in the contexts of our society's established standards. There seems to be a badge of honor attached to being able to do 50 things at once. We somehow seem to derive worth from that premise. Well, it's unhealthy. It's what contributes to stress, anxiety, elevated blood pressure and even depression and a host of other "dis-eases". Don't get caught up in all that. It's not about how much you can do but how well you do. It's about quality not quantity. It's a fact that the brain can really only think of one thing at a time. Work with the natural process of your brain. There is an inner dialogue going on that can be distracting and can scatter the energy. There are many techniques that teach you the discipline that is required for stilling the mind and to help you learn what true concentration really is. I recommend

meditation, or Chi Kung, Yoga, Tai Chi or any one of the contemplative arts as a viable form to enhance self-discipline and awareness.

3. Practice being still, the *Art of Stillness*. Being still without thinking anything. Try it. All the masters have acquired this skill. They can actually sit still and think of no-thing. This is why they are able to do the "mystical" manifestations that we see. Opening a lock with the wave of a hand, or seemingly walk about without being noticed. They know how not to cause ripples in the Universal Energy. They have mastered the Self. They truly can focus on one thing and only one thing at a time. The longer you can sit still and still your mind, the more available energy you have. It is in that discipline that teaches patience, acceptance, and unconditional being. This is a skill that will enhance every aspect of your life. It's a great way to enhance ones' healing techniques as well.

4. Learn to "Let Go". As soon as something, whether it's an old bias, an old emotion, blouse, anything, let go of it. Resolve things in your life as quickly as possible. It will unclutter your mind and your emotions will flow more evenly and smoothly. By learning to, "let go", we also learn to let go of preconceived out come, that is how we "think" it will turn out. If you can't let go then you are still trying to control it. If you are still trying to control things then you close off many pathways of personal and spiritual growth. Let things happen when appropriate to do so.

5. Remember the Law of Coalesce! When you think on something it will attract like thoughts. Twenty seconds of one pure thought attracts an equal amount of pure energy of the same resonance and quality. Each twenty mark increases and multiplies the energy. Can you imagine what you could manifest just by two minutes of pure unadulterated thought!!? This equation works equally for both types of thoughts, positive or negative in origin. Be mindful of what you think on or about. Every action you take

was preceded by a thought. What was the quality of your last thought?

These are some of the techniques that'll help you open up to all your abilities. They are healthy guidelines for life whether you are bending spoons or not. Considering our human brain, the way it functions, teaching by association seems to allow information to adhere and coalesce much more effectively.

## Clarity of Thought

In meta-science related material we hear statements like "clarity" of thought or terms like *concentration of pure thought* or *focus of intent*. What does that all actually mean? It means that the quality of what you think IS what will manifest. THIS IS A VERY IMPORTANT STATEMENT. Why? Because it is the core essence of all manifestation at ANY level in this Universe. You cannot short change the thought process. It is exacting. It measures and applies and extracts the exact measure. Not one ounce more not one ounce less. Clarity and quality of thought are not vague ideas, hints, or themes. They are precise. The best way I can think of to explain the nuance of just how the thought process works is by giving you an example of *manifestation*.

## Psychic Criminology

Since the beginning of time seers and dowsers have been helping to locate missing people and solve crimes. Modern psychic criminology began in the mid-nineteenth century. Joseph R. Buchanan, an American physiologist, coined the term "Psycho-metry". Researchers who followed Buchanan theorized that objects retain imprints of the past and their owners. Psychics who handle objects belonging to crime victims frequently find information that often help solve crimes.

Many professional psychics who work in the field prefer to be called "intuitives" or "viewers". Most work pro bono for law enforcement, although some accept donations from private parties involved in the case.

Lawyers sometimes use psychics in selecting juries and in preparing their cases. Psychics may predict which prospective jurors will be beneficial for a lawyer's client. They may also advise the lawyer when clients or prospective witnesses are lying, or when settlement offers will be made by the other side. The testimony of psychics is inadmissible in court.

## Psychic Reading

One of the most public uses of clairsentient skills is psychic readings. These readings often use tools such as cards, stones, or articles of clothing. Some readings focus on parts of the human body, as in Palmistry or Phrenology. Most people seek psychic readings for information about the future, relationship issues, or communication with departed loved ones.

## Psychic Archeology

The application of clairvoyance and other psychic skills are used in the field of archeology, especially in the location of dig sites and the identification of artifacts. Psychics who are experienced in remote viewing are well-suited to psychic archeology.

## Psychic Attack

A psychic attack is a paranormal assault upon humans or animals that causes physical or mental distress, or even death. Psychic attacks can be originated by direct interaction or through out-of-body projection. They are most effective, or influential, when performed during the waning moon. The moon is said to govern psionic forces.

In magic, the equivalent of a psychic attack is a curse. Some magical rituals involve "sending" in which the spell is delivered to the victim by an animal familiar.

## Can Psionic Powers be used for Detrimental Purposes?

Many traditions teach that psychic abilities can only be used for good purposes, for instance healing. Other harmful applications are said to either not work or to rebound back upon the evil-practitioner. The anthropological literature regarding tribal cultures indicates that the violation of a taboo and the placement of a hex can result in death within a few days. This has been attributed, by modern researchers, to an extreme operation of the stress-response syndrome. We might consider the reported instances of deaths, illness, and accidents from hexes, voodoo, spells, and curses to be the result of suggestion. Although we might just as easily ask ourselves whether, if psi could heal people independently of suggestion, it could not also be used to harm them.

Interestingly, psionic ability has a lot to do with personality alignment. To become good at something you must practice it over and over. Running is a good example. Some people practice short sprints while others practice distance running, like marathons. If these runners were suddenly asked to compete in the opposite form of running than that which they have practiced every day for the past several years, they would probably perform poorly. To perform well against their "running alignment" is difficult.

The same is true with psionic abilities. It is difficult to use psionics for malevolent purposes when they have previously been used for positive purposes. Since most people are innately "good", most people who are Psions have "good" alignment. However, there are always those who choose to use the powers for "less than good" purposes.

Is
There
One?

# Chapter Three

# PHYSICS OF PSIONICS

Although science does not formally acknowledge or support the existence of psionic powers, the physical properties and laws of physics both support and explain the psionic process.

## Energy

Energy can be simply defined as the ability to do work. Power is the amount of energy used. A high-powered device uses a lot of energy in a small amount of time. Most of the energy on Earth comes from the sun, some from the internal mechanisms of the Earth's processes, and the rest from stellar particles. Another form of energy, hydroelectricity is created when the kinetic energy of water is used to turn turbines.

Energy, as defined by $E=MC2$, depends on the mass of the moving object and the square of the velocity of light. This is why you should be more afraid of a small, but very fast particle, than a heavier, slower thrown rock. The energy in the psionic process is often one of vibrating energy waves at various frequencies. The more difficult the skill, the more psionic power is required. Therefore, using psionic powers will cause the user to become tired.

## Force

Currently, physicists have identified four fundamental forces in the universe. These are the gravity force, the nuclear weak force, the nuclear strong force, and the electromagnetic force. A force is any influence which tends to change the motion of an object (cause and effect). In mechanics, forces are seen as the cause of linear motion, whereas the causes of rotational motion are called torques. Forces are inherently vector quantities, requiring vector addition to combine them. The action of forces in causing motion is described by Newton's Laws of Motion.

### Strong Force

The *"strong force"* is strictly an attractive force which acts between nucleons (protons and neutrons). It is the force between color particles. It attracts any combination of protons and neutrons. This is the force that overcomes the repulsive force within an atom due to the electromagnetic force and holds the nucleus together. The strong force actually functions between quarks. It is the residual strong force that causes nucleons to attract. The carrier of this force is the gluon.

### Weak Force

The *"weak force"* is a repulsive force. All the stable matter in the universe appears to be made up of one type of lepton (the electron) and two quarks (the up and down), which compose the neutron and the proton.

## Gravity

Gravity acts between all particles that have mass. Mass attracts other mass with a force that gets weaker as the distance between the masses gets larger. This is true in both physical objects and human relations. The carrier of the gravitational force is the *gravitron*.

## Causes of Motion

Nearly all of what we understand about motion is based on Newton's three "Laws of Motion". Newton's First Law states that an object will continue at rest, or in motion, in a straight line, at constant velocity, unless acted upon by an external force. The influences which cause changes in the motion of objects are forces and torques. The relationship between force, mass, and acceleration is given by Newton's Second Law. Newton's Third Law states that all forces in nature occur in pairs of forces which are *equal in magnitude* and *opposition in direction*. In a more practical application, we refer to this as "cause and effect". Anything (a person or a mind, for example) will continue in a straight line, down a path, until acted on by external forces (a wall, rain, or suggestion).

## Matter Substructure

Because the unit particles of matter are the fundamental units of electrical charge, matter has electrical charge, either positive of negative. Units of matter are themselves only centers of electrical charge, and do not themselves posses mass or energy. The units of matter host energy, but are not made of energy, just electrical charge. The two types of units of matter, positive and negative, are the fundamental units of electrical charge.

## Magnetism

Magnetism is an attracting force. It is polarized, having a positive and negative direction. All rocks have been found to have magnetic properties. The direction of their magnetism is determined at the time of their creation. For example, rocks that form at the poles have a magnetic orientation upward and rocks formed at the equator have a magnetic orientation 90 degrees to the side. This method is used by geologists to determine the exact location a rock was formed on Earth, given its' relative new position as affected by volcanoes, tidal waves, plate shifts, wind storms, human travelers, and so forth. This finding also gives support to the theories of astrology, psycho-metobolic, and psychokinetic.

Human beings have magnetic qualities as well. In human relationships, we are "attracted" to someone, or worse, "repelled" by them. We are attracted to kinds of music, pieces of art, or types of activities. In relationships we are attracted by someone's height, hair color, appearance, personality, or charisma. Perhaps the most powerful human physical expression is the "smile". People will always react to a smile. Try it!

Recent studies have indicated that the human mind can influence a highly magnetized environment, creating the appearance of apparitions in a magnetically charged environment. The human body, as any physical object with mass, has magnetic properties. The uniqueness of the human body is that it contains an electrically charged processing unit, the brain. The uniqueness of the human brain is that it has a natural ability for creativity and focus. Therefore, the human brain is capable of focusing some creative magnetic energy into the environment.

## Electromagnetic and Psionics

*Telekinesis* is the ability to move physical objects in the physical world by psychic means. Some people do have abilities in this area. It seems to be a young man's game and out of reach of the writer who is now a senior citizen. However, these energies are accessible once one has reasonable control of minds, and one can successfully target minds below one's current level. Once one has enough control over minds, psi appears to be a function of Spirit and body working together. Body and Spirit must work as equals to use these energies.

*Electromagnetic Fields and Energies:* The Earth has its own electromagnetic system which can be detected at any time using a compass. Then there are man made energies such as TV, radio and microwaves. A popular theory now is that dowsing works by people being able to detect subtle changes in the Earth's magnetic field. Earth electromagnetic energies make a good bench mark for psychic work as there is nothing psychic about them. However, their interaction with human bodies does cause psionic effects.

*A Faraday Cage* is a six sided box of wire mesh, with all pieces of mesh electrically connected to each other and to earth. This was invented by Michael Faraday (1791-1867, English chemist and physicist who discovered electromagnetic induction). Wire mesh is as efficient in screening out electromagnetic energies as a solid metal box. Professional cages are made out of copper mesh, but some amateurs have been quite successful using galvanized chicken wire mesh. Sitting in a faraday cage has the reputation of inducing mental peace and increased mediumship, but detrimental to physical psi. Hazards have been reported in using them too much. There is a report of a lady who turned her bedroom into a faraday cage, but had to find another bedroom due to mediumistic dreams.

## Origin of the Earth's Magnetic Field

The Earth's magnetic field has many important functions. Not only does it keep us from floating away, it keeps the air we breathe, the water we drink, and all the things we use from floating away. The magnetic field also repels and deflects harmful particles from space, such as solar radiation. The Earth's magnetic field was formed largely from the metal in meteors and other metallic space debris smashing into the Earth. Because metal is heavy it is buried into the center of the Earth. Nearly all the metal on/in Earth is still near the center of the sphere. The daily rotation of the Earth creates a magnetic field, with a polarized north and south direction. However, a hypothetical line drawn from one magnetic pole to the other does not actually pass through the Earth's geographic center.

Magnetic fields from past geographical eras are sometimes preserved in magnetically strata and rocks such as lava as they cool below their Curie points, and their intensities can be measured. Internal molten lava is brought to the surface and creates more land surface as it cools. The land surface on the earth is not recycled as quickly as material in the sea.

Ley Lines are the result of bombardment of the Earth by meteors and other galactic debris. These objects penetrated into the less dense mantle to various depths where they remain. Pieces of meteors often hit the Earth in a line, based on the direction of the meteor and the rotation of the Earth. Over millions of years this debris has produced "hot spots", ley lines. Animals often use these lines as aids in traveling. The ancient Chinese called these Ley Lines "Dragon Tracks".

An examination of the distribution of hot spots over the Earth's surface is interesting. Their distribution is non-random. The bulk of the hot spots lie within an area roughly between 45 degrees north and 45 degrees south latitudes.

These large, long lasting magnetic distorting sources are capable of temporarily over-riding the natural directional polar magnetization effect of the centrifugal force produced by the Earth's spin effects, due to the inherent asymmetry of hot spots. This will cause the needle of a compass to point in the "wrong" direction, or just spin.

## Wave theory

The universe was created by a single entity of energetic matter, which, through spinning and swirling motions, formed two swirls (loops) that together compromised a wave. These two swirls, which are the primary components of every wave, adhere to the following equation:

$$\text{Photon} = \frac{\text{Magnetic (loop)}}{\text{Energetic (loop)}} \qquad \frac{\text{Energetic (loop)}}{\text{Magnetic (loop)}} = 1$$

$$\frac{Mg}{En} = \frac{En}{Mg} \qquad \frac{En}{Mg} = 1$$

This equation also corresponds of the principle of quantum mechanics. This equation holds true for all the formations that exist in the universe. However, in different phases, the proportion between the energetic and magnetic loops varies.

## Definition of Time

Wave theory provides a more natural explanation to Einstein's General Theory of Relativity. Space, energy, and time function as one unit, which constitutes an integral part of energetic matter's activities. In the absence of space and energy, the natural phenomenon of time is both irrelevant and impossible.

Loss of energy means loss of time and space, while an increase in energy is synonymous with larger space and extended time. Time thus depends on the size of and amount of energy in a wave. Hence, when normal energy is distorted, normal perception of time is also distorted. In the human experience, these conditions can easily be seen. When a loss of energy is experienced, such as being tired at the end of a long day, humans often fall into a deep sleep to rest and recover. During this period the internal perception of space and time are greatly diminished.

On the other hand, when humans take caffeine, or its big bad uncle cocaine, energy levels are raised. The internal perception of space and time are greatly increased.

Due to the fact that energy only exists in wave formations (swirls), it appears that time is limited to such formations as well, quant formations (energetic space), and is bound to energetic entities. The phrase "time is ticking away", in essence, means that energy does away with time.

Interestingly, none of the components – *time, space, or energy* – are tangible. In other words, matter is actually virtual, yet there is no denying that it exists. Further, any unit of matter would cease to exist should any one of these elements be removed.

$$Time = \frac{energy \times space}{Oscillation*}$$

\* Oscillation is the frequency of wave rotation relative to other energetic formations.

## Psi balls

*Psi Balls* are quasi-physical constructs that are made by gathering energy at, or between, the hands. Although they are referred to as "Psi Balls", they can actually take any shape or property the Psion chooses. These energy constructs can be any geometric form, color, or density. It all depends on the proficiency of the Psion. Master Psions can cause the energy constructs to curve, arc, bounce, pulse, hover, corner, and even have delayed actions.

Nature produces an electrical phenomena similar to Psi Balls called "ball-lightening". Ball lightening can generate electric currents. Its explosion makes the impression of electric discharge upon many people. Ball lightening is a self-contained, alternating displacement current. Immediately after ball lightening appears, the air is heated due to the polarization current. Appearance of radio-interference proves that ball lightening is an electric current because chemical reactions cannot produce such interference.

Displacement currents have magnetic energy. Self-contained alternating displacement current changes into conduction current. Displacement current, in contrast to conductive current, is not accompanied with heat generation, but only produces magnetic fields. Displacement electric current and conduction current can be direct or alternating.

## Quantum Chromodynamics (QCD)

A major computational breakthrough in the theory of the nuclear strong force was reported in the February 1996 Scientific American. A new particle (glueball) was predicted mathematically and then found in old data where it had been unrecognized. *QCD* is a nonabelian gauge theory best described in terms of the mathematics of fiber bundles in which each space-time point has an internal structure represented by a point on the surface of a hyper-sphere in three complex dimensions. Hadrons are stringy filaments of chromo-electric field with the quarks at the end. The energy of the string is large compared with that of the quarks. A glueball is a closed string with no quarks. This self-interaction is a kind of curvature in internal hyper-sphere space similar to the gravitational curvature in space-time.

## Chapter Four

# PHYSIOLOGY OF PSIONICS

## Metabolism

Two different pathways are involved in the metabolism of glucose; anaerobic and aerobic. The aerobic metabolism of fat serves two main functions; 1. to produce energy from fats (lipids), and; 2. to control membrane permeability, which determines what nutrients enter and what waste products leave the cell. The anaerobic process occurs in the cytoplasm and is only moderately efficient in releasing energy. The aerobic cycle takes place in the mitochondria. It has the greatest release of energy, though it requires oxygen. Aerobic exercise increases psionic ability.

A decrease in psionic skills are *dysaerobic* in nature. For example, when you talk on a mobile phone your voice is transmitted from the antenna as radio frequency radiation (RFR) between 800MHz and 1,990MHz, a frequency range that is right in the middle of microwave frequency. Exposure to this microwave RFR has serious health consequences. There is excessive mortality from brain cancer among wireless phone users as well as intraepithelial tumors.

Many signs point to DNA damage as the likely cause. There is a link between low-intensity microwave and DNA damage in rat brain cells. RFR may not damage DNA, but may somehow hinder the ability of DNA to repair itself when it is damaged by natural causes. Symptoms of "microwave sickness" are dysaerobic in nature.

Symptoms Associated with Dysaerobia
- Fatigue from energy breakdown
- Insomnia
- Allergic sensitivities
- Shortness of breath
- Anxiety
- Schizophrenia
- Manic depression
- Migraine headaches
- Hearing loss
- Multiple sclerosis
- Low cellular potassium, eosinophils, white blood cell count
- Symptoms are worse at night

## Salt Deficiency

Salt deficiency in the diet is a cause of many serious diseases. The healing methods of Hippocrates in the 5th century BC made frequent use of salt. We can not live without sodium chloride. There is not enough natural salt in our foods, so we must supplement it in our diet. However, the salt we often use in our diet is not appropriate. During the refining process the sodium chloride evaporates and sodium hydroxate is left. Sodium hydroxate irritates the system and does not satisfy the body's hunger and need for sodium chloride.

The problem with "salt" is not the salt itself, but the condition of the salt we eat. Our regular table salt is not like sea salt. Pure unrefined sea salts contain essential amounts of sodium chloride, which is one of the 12 daily essential minerals. The common table salt we use for cooking has only two or three chemical elements. Seawater salt has 84 chemicals. This causes the body to become imbalanced and more susceptible to disease. Twenty-seven percent of the bodys' salt is in the bones, twentytwo percent is water. Natural salt, sodium chloride, dissolves in water and can therefore dissolve in our body. The manufacturing companies dry their salt in huge kilns with temperatures reaching 1200 degrees F, changing the salt's chemical structure, which in turn adversely affects the human body.

When salt crystals are heated they create a natural energy field. This energy field can help neutralize the positive ions and electromagnetic field frequencies. This can help with relaxation, strengthen the immune system, the heart, the adrenals, and the thyroid. Inhaled salts have an anti-inflammatory effect and can provide relief for respiratory symptoms. Crystal salt is one of only a few minerals whose atomic structure is bound electrically, not molecularly. This characteristic enables the crystal to change back and forth from crystalline to liquid state. This natural ionization creates an electric charge, a pure natural energy vibration.

## Salt is effective in:

- Stabilizing irregular heart beats
- Extracting excess acidity from the cells in the body
- Generating hydroelectric energy in the cells of the body
- Helping nerve cells' communication and information processing
- Clearing the lungs of mucus and sticky phlegm
- Clearing up catarrh and congestion in the sinus
- A strong natural antihistamine
- Prevention of muscle cramps
- Making the structure of bones firm
- Sleep regulation
- Vitally needed in the treatment of diabetes
- Salt is a natural hypnotic

## Microwaves

Microwaves are very short waves of electromagnetic energy that travel at the speed of light (186,282 miles per second). The Nazis originally developed microwaves for use in their mobile support operation, They created "radiomissor" cooking ovens to be used for the invasion of Russia to conserve the use of cooking fuels. In our modern technological age, microwaves are used to relay long distance telephone signals, television programs, and to heat up food.

Radiation is an electro-magnetic wave emitted by the atoms and molecules of a radioactive substance as a result of nuclear decay. The wavelength determines the type of radiation; radio, X-ray, ultraviolet, visible, infrared, etc. Amplitude determines the extent of movement measured from the starting point. Cycle determines the unit of frequency, such as cycles per second, Hertz, Hz, or cycles/second.

Microwaves are a form of electromagnetic energy, like light waves or radio waves, and occupy a part of the electromagnetic spectrum of power, or energy. Frequency determines the number of occurrences within a given time period, the number of occurrences of a recurring process per unit of time, or the number of repetitions of cycles per second.

Of all natural substances, which are polar, the oxygen of water molecules reacts most sensitively to microwaves. Because the electrochemical body is water based in nature, any force that disrupts or changes human electrochemical events will affect the physiology of the body.

People who spend a lot of time with television, computers, cell phones, and microwave ovens will likely experience "microwave sickness" symptoms. People who always carry cell phones on their body will likely experience headaches, or a center of pain radiating from the area of the body they carry their cell phone. The first sign of "microwave sickness" is low blood pressure and slow pulse. Signs of dysanerobic are common.

Other symptomatic characteristics include chronic excitation of the sympathetic nervous system (stress syndrome) and high blood pressure. Other characteristics include headaches, dizziness, eye pain, sleep-lessness, irritability, anxiety, stomach pain, nervous tension, hair loss, inability to concentrate, and an increased incident of appendices, cataracts, reproductive problems, and cancer.

- A breakdown of the human "life-energy field"
- A degeneration of the cellular voltage
- A degeneration and destabilization of external energy
- A degeneration and destabilization of internal cellular membrane
- Degeneration and circuit breakdowns of electrical nerve impulses within the cerebrum
- A degeneration and breakdown of nerve electrical circuits and loss of energy field symmetry in the neuro-plexuses, both in front and the rear of the central and autonomic nervous systems

- Loss of balance and circuiting of the bioelectric strengths within the ascending reticular activating system (the system which controls the function of consciousness).
- High levels of brainwave disturbance in the alpha, theta, and delta wave signal patterns
- Loss of memory, loss of ability to concentrate, suppressed emotional threshold, deceleration of intellective processes, and interruptive sleep.
- Causes immune system deficiencies through lymph gland and blood serum alterations

## Limbic System

The *limbic system* is made up of the amygdala, hippocampus, hypothalamus, thalamus, putamen, and caudate nucleus.

The amygdala has three parts. One part stimulates fear, producing a feeling of panic combined with flight. A second region results in outbursts of rage. When the third area is stimulated, people experience a warm, floating feeling, and can demonstrate excessively friendly behavior and appeasement.

Facial expressions of emotion are very similar all over the world, i.e. a smile. This suggests that the neural circuits that create and respond to emotions are hard wired into the brain rather than molded by culture. There are five basic expressions; disgust, fear, anger, sadness, and happiness. The thousands of other faces we have are blends of these five. Note that only one of these expressions are commonly considered positive.

Fear is identified by the amygdala. Disgust activates the anterior insular cortex, and is stimulated by offensive stimuli. The sight of an expression of intense disgust lights up the limbic system. This suggest that when you look at a person who is showing mild disgust, you register it with your conscious brain only. But if the person's expression changes to intense disgust, it effectively causes you to experience the disgust, as well as recognizing it in the other person.

Hence, the greater the delivered expression, the greater the effect of upon the receiver. The modification made by the Psion is that instead of actually feeling and internalizing these expressions, the Psion acts as a sender. They create the energy of the expression and focus it into another, without directly being affected by the energy.

## Frontal Lobe

The *frontal lobes* are areas of the brain where ideas are created, plans constructed, and thoughts joined with associations to form new memories. This brain region is the location of consciousness. Self-awareness is active and emotions are transformed here. If you were to draw a "You are here X" on your mind map, it would be on the frontal brain lobe; the "third eye". High-quality consciousness (awareness, perception, self-awareness, attention, and reflection) requires a fair amount of frontal lobe activity.

The frontal lobes are connected by numerous neural pathways to the other cortical areas and to the limbic region. These paths are two-way. Information must flow into the frontal lobes in order for them to function. A heavy input of negative emotion can inhibit activity in the frontal lobes.

The flow of neural traffic is mediated by the neurotransmitters dopamine, seratona, and adrenaline. Any disturbance to these chemicals, or damage to the tissue that is sensitive to them, can have negative effects on the way we think, feel, and behave.

Emotional stimuli are registered by the amygdala. Conscious emotion is created both by direct signals from the amygdala to the frontal cortex, and indirectly through the hypothalamus. These changes are then fed back to the somatosensory cortex, which feeds the information forward to the frontal cortex where it is interpreted as emotion.

## Brian Area Disorders

There are mental health and physical damage issues that can create perceptions which are similar to psionic skills, but are actually the result of mental disorder. For example, damage, or influence to the frontal lobe, reduces the brain's ability to distinguish between externally and internally generated stimuli. Damage, or influence to the occipio-parietal area, may make objects seem to appear or disappear due to *simultagnosia*, the inability to hold two objects in vision at the same time.

Stimulation of the temporal lobe, may produce intense flash-backs and feelings of a "presence". Stimulation of the limbic system produces intense feelings of joy, and a feeling of being in the presence of God. Religious visions are likely to occur. Stimulation of the auditory cortex produces hallucinatory voices.

Over stimulation of the right hemisphere (visual shape area) may trigger the perception of ghostly outlines. The reason ghost are more likely seen at night is that in the absence of competing visual stimuli, the brain picks up the shadow in the corner and molds it into a sinister figure, brought up from the memory storage area. A disturbance of the parietal/sensory cortex often result in the perception of a spectral version of oneself (doppelgangers).

## God

Religious belief and experience are usually regarded as beyond scientific exploration, yet neurologists have located an area in the temporal lobe of the brain that appears to produce intense feelings of spiritual transcendence, combined with a sense of some mystical presence. Neurologists have even managed to reproduce such feelings in otherwise unreligious people by stimulating this area. EEGs show a classic slow-wave seizure spike over the temporal lobe at the precise time of the experience. It is theorized that if God exists, He must have created us with some biological mechanism with which to understand Him. You can get your "God" experience from a well-placed electrode.

## Meditation

Meditation is often described by proponents as a type of intense inward concentration that allows focus on the senses. Step back from your thoughts and feelings, and perceive each moment as a unique event.

Mediation can be seen as a form of mental martial arts. We are naturally reactive to our emotions and thoughts. They attack us and we kick and yell back at them. In meditation, we learn to sidestep out of the way. We learn how to keep ourselves centered so that we are no longer at the mercy of our own thoughts.

Concentrative Meditation, i.e. Transcendental Meditation (TM), uses a picture, a word, an object, or a sensation to focus the mind. If your mind drifts, you can refocus your attention on the object.

Mindful Meditation, i.e. active meditation used in Mikkyo, is more complex. Instead of focusing on a single sensation or object, our thoughts, feelings, and images are allowed to float through the mind. The mind becomes aware, mindful, of certain patterns. The result is direct influence (cause and effect) on the patterns of images.

**Breathing**

Deep breathing is one of the simplest ways to relax. When you slow down your breathing and focus your attention in your belly, it has a profound physiological and psychological effect. Deep abdominal breathing relaxes tight chest muscles and opens up blood vessels so the heart can pump more efficiently. It opens and relaxes the blood vessels in the brain so that you can think clearly and stay calm in a stressful situation.

## Chapter Five

# BIOMAGNETISM:
# THE FOUNDATION OF LIFE

Scientists have been extensively researching organisms that have the ability to produce the ferromagnetic mineral "magnetite". Magnetite is a black mineral form of iron oxide that crystallizes in the nucleus. Magnetite is a kind of mechanoreceptor. It is a mix of iron and iron oxide ($Fe_3O_4$), which is strongly magnetic. Some varieties, known as lodestone, are natural magnets. These were used as compasses in the ancient world. Magnetite is also found in the animal and human bones and brain.

The discovery of a biomagnetic material with ferromagnetic properties, like magnetite, leads to the understanding as to why some animals have the ability to detect magnetic fields. The search for bioorganic magnetite in human tissues has not been conclusive until the past decade with invention and use of high-resolution transmission electron microscopy and electron diffraction on human brain tissues such as the cerebral cortex, cerebellum, and meninges. These areas have been found to have identified magnetite-maghemite crystals.

These magnetite crystals are organized into linear, membrane, biomagnetic chains, a few micrometers in length, with up to 80 crystals per chain. Furthermore, individual crystals have their polar magnetism aligned along the length of the chain. Ferromagnetic crystals interact more than a million times more strongly with magnetic fields than do diamagnetic or paramagnetic materials. All the magnetite crystals that have been examined to date are a single magnetic domain, which means that they are uniformly and stably magnetized and have a maximum magnetic moment per unit volume.

All organisms appear to have some magnetite. Magnetite has been found in animals that navigate by compass directions such as bees, birds, and fish. Magnetite can turn simple bacteria into swimming needles that orient themselves with respect to the earth's magnetic fields. Research has shown that magnetite is produced by the cells of organisms when needed. Animals with advanced intelligence can directly tune into this direction-finding information.

In the human brain, pyramidal cells are arranged in layers in the cortex of the cerebra. The pyramidal cells act as electromagnetic cells immersed in extra-cellular tissue and seems to operate in the fashion of a liqoscillator in response to different light commands, or light pulses which, influences the orientation of every molecule within the body. Psions are both generator and capacitors.

Biogravitational encoded switches in the brain allow a liquid network to release ions that induce the surrounding coiled dendrites. Electrical impulses from a neuron, on reaching the coil of the surrounding cell, generate a micro amperage magnetic field, causing the liquid crystal in the pyramidal cell to be activated, in a very unusual way. This ultra thin crystal becomes a piezoelectric oscillator, producing a circular polarized light pulse that travels throughout the body, or travels as a traverse photonic bundle of energy. This is the physiology of auras.

In publication by The Academy of Science, it was stated that "under present biological conditions, evolution development in living bodies from earliest inception follows unicellular semi conductivity, as a living piezoelectric matrix, through stages which permeate primitive basic tissue (glia, satellite, and Schwann cells) to be supportive in the human system where the primary source is electrical. This has been established in bone growth response to mechanical stress and to fractures which have been demonstrated to have characteristics of control systems using electricity".

Ongoing research has shown that bone has electrical properties. The bone marrow is a biphasic (two-part) semiconductor, i.e. a crystalline solid with an electrical conductivity. Mechanical stress on the bone thus produces a piezoelectric signal. The signal is biphasic, switching polarity with each stress-and-release. The strength of the signal tells the bone cells how strong the stress is, and its polarity tells them what direction it comes from. Estrogenic (bone forming) cells, which have been shown to have a negative potential, would be stimulated to grow more bone.

**Biofeedback**

Biofeedback is a training technique in which people are taught to improve their health and performance by using signals from their own body. The term "biofeedback" first appeared in the late 1960's, at a time when most facets of technologically assisted self-regulation were vague and unexplored. Its' design is to describe laboratory procedures (developed in the 1940's) that trained research subjects to alter brain activity, blood pressure, muscle tension, heart rate and other bodily functions that are not normally called voluntary.

In "conditioning" biofeedback, there is no reliance on maintaining any particular state of mind. In fact, behavioralists have shown that positive changes do occur without the subject even knowing that the changes are being encouraged. Interestingly, volition is paradoxical, in that the harder you try the more you fail.

Researchers in psychoneuroimmunology have shown that individuals can use mental imagery to influence their own physiological sates. Controlling emotions is effectively the reverse of the process required to feel them. When the emotional information reaches the frontal cortex, it is placed in context, and a rational plan of action is conceived to cope. This process is sometimes called preverbal imagery, a form of bio-feedback.

### Smell

Humans have always used forms of smell ("Aromatherapy", Rene-Maurice Gattefosse, 1927) for rituals and in healing. In the eleventh century A.D., European healers began working with essential oils, liquids, and smells from plants. This technique was introduce to Europe by crusaders returning from the Middle East. It wasn't until the lat 1980's that Americans began to use fragrant smell as medicine.

Smell acts directly on the brain like a drug. Research has

found that people who lost their sense of smell seem to have a higher incidence of psychiatric problems, such as anxiety and depression. Brain wave frequency research shows that smelling lavender increases alpha waves in the back of the brain, which are associated with relaxation. Jasmine increases beta waves in the front of the brain, which is associated with more alertness. Pleasant orders mainly light up the frontal lobes' smell area on the right-hemisphere. Unpleasant odors activate the amygdala and the cortex in the temporal lobe.

## Sound

What you hear, listen to, especially music, impacts your physical and mental health. The type and volume of music listened to will produce different levels of chemicals in the brain. Sound can release energy in the body to help healing or cause trauma. There are a number of research studies showing that sound can ease pain, improve memory, and reduce stress. Ultrasound machines are used to help heal soft-tissue injuries and to take diagnostic photographs. Sound waves can be used to destroy large, solid objects.

All sound comes in energy waves. These waves have a number of variables that give sound a unique quality. Among them are velocity, the speed at which the waves travel; frequency, which is the number of waves per second that an object produces; and intensity, which is a measure of a sound's loudness.

Our body's main sensor is the ear. The skin, bones, fluid, and nerves in the ear help collect sound waves and send impulses to the brain, in the hypothalamus. The brain reacts to these impulses and sends out instructions that help control heart rate, breathing rate, and so on. The heart will nearly always speed up or slow down to match the rhythm of a nearby sound. This process is called entrainment. Sound waves can entrain the brain wave functions in a matter of seconds.

Vibrations from sound waves can have a direct impact on

individual body parts. Science has shown that every atom vibrates, emitting sound waves, even though they are too faint for us to hear. Since body parts are made up of atoms, they all produce sound waves. When we contract a disease our normal body sound (and color vibration) is disrupted. By directing healthy sound waves at the body, restoring the natural rhythms facilitates healing. This technique is called cymatic therapy. It is used by holistic practitioners such as acupuncturists and osteopaths.

Sound waves can balance energy centers (charkas) in the body, thereby promoting health. Chakras control function and energy flow in different organs of the body. Each chakra vibrates at a specific frequency that relates to a note on the scale. When there are disruptions to the chakras caused by stress, disease, or other factors, the frequencies are thrown off. By applying specific sounds, or music to the body, the charkas can be returned to normal, and the body will heal itself.

Some music may make you smarter. Research has found that college students who listen to Mozart for 10 minutes a day scored higher on intelligence tests than students who listened to relaxation tapes or meditated quietly. Pythagoras developed prescriptions of music for his ailing students. He told them which sounds would help them to work, relax, sleep, and wake better. The Bible tells that David played music on his harp to ease the madness of King Saul. Buddhist Monks, Native Americans, and other cultures around the world use musical tones for different purposes.

Music is often used to communicate with people who have a communication disabilities, such as autistic children, Alzheimer's patients, and TBI. Big band music seems to work best for increasing alertness and recall of past events. Soft music makes work seem less difficult and allow people to work longer. Listening to hard rock increases the heart rate and work periods are usually shorter and more chaotic. Much of what we call 'New

Age' music is composed specifically for therapeutic use. This music has a carefully timed beat and a sequence of tones that is supposed to stimulate relaxation.

A new branch of sound therapy, called music tautology, seeks to ease the emotional and physical suffering of terminally ill patients. This technique uses harp and vocal music similar to that of which medieval monks used to comfort people who where dying. The key to these techniques is that they involve whole body resonating entrainment. The harp is held next to the body when played. The harp player both hears the sound and feels the vibration.

Research has shown that 'Rock' music will weaken muscle strength while people are listening to it. Many times people will listen to hard, loud music and they think it is relaxing them. But what it is really doing is just distracting part of the brain. They are not getting any physiological benefit. They are just trying to block out whatever is making them tense.

The sounds most physiologically and mentally suited for humans are natural sounds, such as leaves rustling in the breeze, wind blowing through the trees, or flowing water. These are sounds that trigger healthy brain function, gives us mental balance, and physiological health. Taking a walk in the quit woods is probably healthier than going to a high-tech gym.

## Binaural Beats

Binaural beats are auditory brainstem responses which originate in the superior olivary nucleus of each hemisphere. They result from the interaction of two different auditory impulses, originating in opposite ears, below 1000Hz and which differ in frequency between one and 30 Mhz. For example, if a pure tone of 400 Mhz is presented to the right ear and a pure tone of 410 Mhz is presented simultaneously to the left ear, an amplitude modulated standing wave of 10 Mhz, the difference between the two tones, is experienced as the two wave form mesh in and out of phase within the superior olivary nuclei. This binaural beat is not heard in the ordinary sense of the word (the human range of hearing is from 20 to 20,000MHz). It is perceived as an auditory beat and theoretically can be used to entertain specific neural rhythms through the frequency following response (FFR), the tendency of cortical potential to entrain, or resonate, at the frequency of an external stimulus. Thus, it's theoretically possible to utilize a specific binaural beat frequency as a consciousness management technique to entrain a specific cortical rhythm.

Binaural beats were discovered in 1839 by H. W. Dove, a German scientist. The human ability to "hear" binaural beats appears to be the result of evolutionary adaptation. Many evolved species can detect binaural beats because of their brain structure. The frequencies at which binaural beats can be detected change depending upon the size of the species' cranium. In the human, binaural beats can be detected when carrier waves are below approximately 1000 Hz (Oster,1973). Below 1000 Hz the wave length of the signal is longer than the diameter of the human skull. Thus, signals below 1000 Hz curve around the skull.

The same effect can be observed with radio wave propagation. Lower-frequency (longer wave length) radio waves, such as AM radio, travel around the earth over and in between mountains and structures. Higher-frequency (shorter wave length) radio waves (such as FM radio, TV, and microwaves) travel in a straight line and can't curve around the earth. Mountains and structures block these high-frequency signals. Because frequencies below 1000 Hz curve around the skull, incoming signals below 1000 Hz are heard by both ears. But due to the distance between the ears, the brain "hears" the inputs from the ears as out of phase with each other. As the sound wave passes around the skull, each ear gets a different portion of the wave.

It is this waveform phase difference that allows for accurate location of sounds below 1000 Hz. Audio direction finding at higher frequencies is less accurate than it is for frequencies below 1000 Hz. At 8000 Hz the pinna (external ear) becomes effective as an aid to localization. In summary it is the ability of the brain to detect a waveform phase difference. This is what enables the brain to perceive binaural beats.

The difference between the signals waxes and wanes as the two different input frequencies mesh in and out of phase. As a result of these constantly increasing and decreasing differences, an amplitude-modulated standing wave, the binaural beat, is heard. The binaural beat is perceived as a fluctuating rhythm at the frequency of the difference between the two auditory inputs. Binaural beat are generated in the brainstem's superior livery nucleus, the first site of contra lateral integration in the auditory system. Frequency-following response originates from the inferior follicular. This activity is conducted to the cortex where it can be recorded by scalp electrodes.

## The Frequency-Following Response Effect (FFR)

The binaural beat appears to be associated with an electro-encephalographic (EEG) frequency-following response (FFR) in the brain.

Studies have demonstrated the presence of FFR to auditory stimuli, recorded in the human brain. The EEG activity is termed frequency-following response because its period corresponds to the fundamental frequency of the stimulus. Audio embedded messages with binaural beats are often combined with various meditation techniques, as well as positive affirmations and visualization. Binaural-beat stimulation appears to encourage access to altered states of consciousness.

## Altered States

A trance state is one type of an altered state of consciousness that is between sleep and wakefulness. Binaural beats can easily be heard at the low frequencies below 30 Hz. This level is characteristic of the EEG spectrum. This perceptual phenomenon of binaural beating and the objective measurement of the frequency-following response indicate conditions which facilitate entertainment of brain waves and altered states of consciousness. Music, relaxation exercises, guided imagery, and verbal suggestion have all been used to enhance the state-changing effects of the binaural beat.

## Brain Waves and Consciousness

Consciousness is the result of electromagnetic neurological activity. There is, however, growing observations to the contrary. There is no neuropsychological research which conclusively shows that the higher levels of mind (intuition, insight, creativity, imagination, intent, will, spirit, or soul) are located in brain tissue (Hunt, 1995). The human mind has been found to continue to work in spite of the brain's reduced activity under anesthesia. Mind-consciousness appears to be a field phenomenon which interfaces with the body and the neurological structures of the brain. This field can not be measured with current instruments. On the other hand, the electrical potentials of brain waves can be measured and easily quantified.

## Synchronized Brain Waves

Synchronized brain waves are associated with meditative and hypnologic states. An audio tape with embedded binaural beats has the ability to induce and improve states of consciousness. Each ear is hardwired to both hemispheres of the brain. Each hemisphere has its own *olivary* nucleus (sound-producing center) which receives signals from each ear. So there are two separate standing waves entraining portions of each hemisphere to the same frequency. The binaural beats contribute to the hemispheric synchronization and also enhanced through the increase of cross-colossal communication between the left and right hemisphere of the brain.

## Sodium/Potassium Ratio in Theta Brain Waves

The brain cells reset sodium and potassium ratios when the brain is in Theta. After an extended state in the Beta level the ratio between potassium and sodium is out of balance. This causes "mental fatigue". The sodium and potassium levels are involved in osmosis, which is a chemical process that transports chemicals into and out of brain cells. A brief period in Theta (5–15 minutes) can restore the ratio to normal, resulting in mental refreshing.

## Resonant "Entrainment" of Oscillating Systems

Resonant "entrainment" of oscillating systems is a well-understood principle within the physical sciences. If a tuning fork designed to produce a frequency of 440 MHZ is struck, causing it to oscillate, and then brought into the vicinity of another 440 Hz tuning fork, the second tuning fork will begin to oscillate. The first tuning fork is said to have entrained the second, or caused it to resonate.

The physics of entrainment apply to bios stems as well. Of interest here are the electromagnetic brain waves. The electro-chemical activity of the brain results in the production of electromagnetic wave forms which can be objectively measured with sensitive equipment. Brain waves change frequencies based on neural activity within the brain. Because neural activity is electrochemical, brain function can be modified through the introduction of specific chemicals (drugs), by altering the brain's electromagnetic environment through induction, or through resonant entrainment techniques.

In personal relationships, we refer to two friends or mates as "thinking as one", "hearts beating together", or "on the same page." Many psionic skills work through resonant brain entrainment. Through brain entraining, the Psion learns to perceive ever smaller vibrations. The Psion can either sync to these vibrations (input) or cause them to vibrate differently (output). The expression "Great minds think alike" really means "I have finally figured out a way to entrain you to think like me and this statement is a reinforcer so you will continue to be entrained so and I won't have to use as much energy to entrain you the next time."

## Chapter Six

# BRAIN WAVES

*Gamma* – brain waves associated with ESP, anxiety, and psychotic disorders.

*Beta* – brain wave level associated with alertness and attentive behavior.

*Alpha* – slow brain waves; resting; daydreams; brain wave level associated with sensory processing disorders, reading and speech disorders, anger, aggression, and dissociative disorders.

*Theta* – stage between sleeping and conscious; awareness; brain wave levels often associated with true depression.

*Delta* – resting sleep; the entire brain oscillates in a gentle rhythm and shows less activity in the limbic system; produces neurotransmitters.

*Sub-Delta* – frequencies can affect both dissociative mind states and cerebral blood flow.

Brain wave frequencies are critical to the functions of psionic ability. Each psionic skill is a function of a specific brain wave frequency, or specific cycling among frequencies. Lower theta and alpha brain wave frequencies are closely associated with broad characteristics of hypnotism, illusions, and hallucinations. In hypnosis, there is an increase in activity in the motor and sensory area, suggesting heightened mental imagery. There is increased blood flow in the right anterior cingulated cortex, suggesting that attention is focused on internal events.

With "Schizophrenia" there is a lack of activity in the frontal lobes in which consciousness is disturbed or decreased. The anterior cingulated cortex, the area which distinguishes between external and internal stimuli, is under-active, which is one reason schizophrenics confuse their own thoughts with outside voices.

Dreaming, vivid visual dreams, light up the visual cortex. Activity is decreased in the *dorsolateral* prefrontal cortex, the area of waking thought and reality testing (beta). Nightmares trigger brain wave activity in the *amygdala* and the *hippocampus*.

During meditation, people in self-induced states of passive attention tend to turn off areas of the brain normally associated with seeking stimuli, including the parietal, anterior, and premotor cortexes. However, active and interactive meditation techniques can increase the stimuli processing areas of the brain.

The alpha/theta wave stimulation significantly helps calm people down and has been shown to improve sports performance. Increasing the stimulation frequency can help increase cognitive function and to treat slow brain wave disorders such as PMS, chronic fatigue, fibromyalgia, closed-head injury, and ADD.

While faster brain wave frequencies, like those in the upper beta to gamma brain are often found in other psi skills like ESP and powerful psionic attacks. Remember though, everything in the universe is balance, or has its counter archetype, the yin and yang. As gamma wave frequencies are often required to perform many psionic abilities, it is also the brain wave frequency of many psychiatric disorders. So be careful in what you want, you just may get it.

When humans are in the analytical thought pattern, trying to classify, sort, define, measure, explain, list, and all those other task oriented verbs, they are in beta brain wave frequencies. Basically, only "automatic" psi skills will engage at lower beta levels. Many consciously directed psionic skills begin in upper Beta levels.

Automatic psi skills are those characteristics that are always operating on low levels. These would include basic scanning for psionic sources and attacks, aura emanations, and protective shield, to name a few. This provides some of the answers to why most people have difficulty performing psionic skills and how, when actually achieved, may be harmful.

## Brian Hemispheres

Left brain activity is associated with language arts, such as reading, and talking. Stimulation of the left brain hemisphere often reduces anxiety. Grief is often reduced by high levels of left-brain activity. This inhibits the emotional response of the left brain. It also helps to alleviate emotions to the cortical level where they can be consciously processed.

Right brain activities often just happen. These activities include facial recognition, recognizing familiar geography, recognizing the number of items in a group, recognizing shapes and colors, etc. Right brain works with wholes and the left brain works with details. Psi is said to be located in the right side of the brain. Psychics and clairvoyants have highly developed right brain abilities and they use this facility to assist them in paranormal activities.

## Clairsentience

Clairsentience, also know as psychometry, is the ability to hold an object or touch someone and sense the energy surrounding that person, place, or thing. A clairsentient is an individual who is empathetic and senses energies. Energies can be light or heavy, smooth or abrasive, prickly or gentle, peaceful and airy or 'good or bad'. For example, when sensing a negative situation a clairsentient may feel sick, while a positive experience may feel like butterflies in the stomach, or a sense of feeling safe, peaceful and light. Learning to discern positive and negative energies can make all the difference when making decisions in life.

Spiritual advisors and counselors use clairsentience to feel and sense the information and thought-forms in energy fields. The information about the nature of energies is revealed in colors, lightness, darkness, or emotions such as joy or sadness. Sometimes clairsentients experience a sense of movement or stillness, relaying past, present and future life events. This ability is known to be essential for healers, counselors, therapists, or anyone who works with people, especially a psychic or spiritual advisor.

We are all born with this particular psionic ability. It's learning to regulate and protect the ability of sensing moods and emotions that's the tricky part! Aside from being honest and naïve, as children we are very open and tuned into the psionic world. As we grow older and experience life, to avoid trauma or negative experiences, we develop a 'thick skin', sheltering ourselves as we begin to interact with people other than the familiar circle of family and friends. These psychic ability are often unconsciously left on the shelf, but fortunately they can be restored later in life by spiritual development or during life-altering experiences.

To use clairsentience for yourself, or improve your

connection with clairsentients who can use this gift on your behalf, it is important to 'listen' to your internal feelings, impressions and sensations. Be aware of and communicate the physical and emotional responses from your 'gut' instincts. By using clairsentience you can make sound decisions in all facets of life from love and relationships to career and spiritual development.

Clairsentience manifests as brief smells, sounds, or sights. These sensations are either just out of normal sensory range (such as just around a corner or on the other side of a door, or just over a hilltop), or are connected in some very familiar way to the psychic. A psychic child, for example, might "overhear" his mother talking about him while she is visiting a neighbor, or might "just know" that his older brother was hiding up in the hayloft, without ever seeing or hearing him. This kind of "sixth sense" is often confused with latent manifestations of ESP, since the two are often indistinguishable to inexperienced latent psychics. The two are very different in actuality. ESP is an added "sense" which manifests, especially among latent psychics, as an intrusion onto the normal physical senses. Clairsentience will not detect anything that the Psion's normal senses would not detect if the psychic were present at another location.

*Sense Extension* is the ability to extend ones senses a short distance from one's body in order to overcome some barrier to normal sensing. In order to use Sense Extension, only barriers to sensing other than distance may limit the psychic. For example, a Psion is hiding behind a door. By using Sense Extension, the psychic can see what is on the other side of the door, or even what is in the next room or on the next floor, because if the intervening door, walls, or ceiling/floor were not in the way, the Psion would be able to see that far. The senses of hearing, smell, and even touch can be similarly extended (although extending the sense of touch has a much more limited application - feeling the texture and shape of something without removing the covering or wrapping, for example).

*Sense Projection* is the ability to project one's senses far away from one's body. In order to do so, the Psion must meet one of two criteria. The Psion must be very familiar with a specific location, or must be very familiar with a specific person or object. If the Psion can locate a person using ESP, the difficulty for using Sense Projection is reduced.

Examples of experiencing other realities or entities through one or more of the five senses are...

- A tickling sensation on the hand or face during meditation.
- A pressure on the top of the head when talking or connecting with a Spirit.
- Hairs on the back of the neck standing on end when a spirit is near.
- A sensation in the left side of the face when talking with a spirit.
- A floral smell... like gardenias.
- A movement as a flick of white, purple, or blue light.
- Seeing shadows in the periphery of your field of vision.
- Funny how smokers–especially cigar smokers–can be experienced as spirits by the smell of a "good cigar"!

## Telepathy

Telepathy is the reception of knowledge without the use of the five common senses.

## Imagery

Imagery is the language that the mind uses to communicate with the body. Images aren't always visual. They can be sounds, tastes, smells, or a combination of senses. Unfortunately, many of the images popping into our heads do more harm than good. In fact, the most common imagery is worry. When we worry, what we worry about exists only in our imagination. The average person has 10,000 thoughts, or images, like these careening through their mind every day. At least half of those thoughts are negative. A steady dose of worry and other negative images can alter your physiology and make you more susceptible to a range of ailments, ranging from acne to ulcers.

Imagery has been considered a healing tool. It is used by all of the world's cultures and is an integral part of many religions. Hippocrates, believed that images release spirits (chemicals) in the brain that effect parts of the body. He also thought that a strong image of a disease is enough to cause its symptom. Imagery may produce a disease, or it may cure a disease.

Early psychologists, like Sigmund Freud and Carl Jung, treated patients with imagery. However, imagery was largely ignored in the United States until 1970, when O. Carl Simmonton, M.D., a radiation oncologist began using it in the early 1970's. He found that people with cancer, who used imagery in conjunction with medical treatment, lived twice as long as those who used medical care alone. When you can learn to direct and control the images in your head, you can help your body heal itself.

## How Imagery Works

The brain reacts the same way to an imagined sensation as to a real one. Imagery is like reality in the sense that if you look at activity in the brain when you're imagining something, it is strikingly similar to the activity that occurs when you're perceiving reality.

Images are formed as a result of electrochemical reactions in the limbic system, a portion of the brain that processes emotions such as pleasure, pain, and anger. As these images arise in the limbic system, they are interpreted by the cerebral cortex. The cerebral cortex is involved in higher brain function like reasoning and memory. Without the cerebral cortex, these images would be meaningless to us.

The limbic system is connected to the hypothalamus, a portion of the brain that regulates body temperature, heart rate, hunger, thirst, sleeping, and sexual arousal. The limbic system is connected to the pituitary gland, which monitors hormones.

After you imagine yourself doing something, your brain triggers the release of nerve impulses, chemicals, and hormones from the hypothalamus and pituitary gland that affect every cell in your body. In return, the cells send signals back to the brain that make the experience seem more vivid and cause the mind to release more chemicals to sustain that image. So, for better or worse, nearly every image has an effect on your body.

If you can learn to control the images in your mind instead of letting them control themselves, they can have a positive, long-term effect on your health and well-being. It is difficult to master. It is a matter of practice. Everyone can successfully use imagery. It's a question of patience and persistence. It's just like learning to master anything else. You put in the time, you put in the discipline, you get good direction from a master teacher, and you can achieve your goal. Initially, Imagery should be practiced for 15 to 20 minutes a day to ensure that you are doing it properly. As you become more skilled and comfortable with the techniques, you will be able to do it for just a few minutes at a time as needed throughout the day. To improve the quality of your images, become a keen observer of life.

**Exercise**

Take a few moments to relax. When the physical body is relaxed, you do not need to be in such conscious control of your mind. Loosen clothing. Lie down or sit in a comfortable chair. Once you feel comfortable gradually direct your mind toward the ailment you are concerned about. If several images come to mind, choose one and stick with it for that session. If you jump from image to image, it will likely break your concentration and make it more difficult for the imagery to work for you. On the other hand, if no images come to mind, focus on a different sensation. At the end of each session imagine that your ailment is completely cured. This creates and internal blueprint that the body can follow to help you heal. At the end of your sessions, take a few more breaths and picture yourself tracing your path back to becoming aware of our surroundings. You may want to sketch a picture of the image you used to help recall it in the future.

## CIA and Mind Control

Since its inception, the "CIA" has been studying the practice and implementation of mind control for a variety of purposes. Officially, the CIA has listed three objectives in their study of mind control. The first is to construct a "brain map" and then use it to control the human bodily functions. Body functions are controlled by various locations in the brain. By electrically stimulating the brain in precise points, emotional feelings such as fear, anxiety, and anger, can be stimulated. Second, based on the brain map research, develop methods of using radio or electrical signals to remotely control animal's brain functions. Production capability was achieved in 1961. 3rd, adapt remote control techniques developed on animals, for eventual use on humans. Current experiments demonstrate the successful use of lasers on the brain of a fly can be used to control the fly's actions.

## Electromagnetic Weapons

From 1965 through 1970, Defense Advanced Projects Research Agency (DAPRA), (80% funded by the military) operated project PANDORA to study the health and psychological effects of low intensity microwaves. Mind control technologies such as microwave voice devices, mind machines, and ELF devices (extreme low frequency) waves can be used to implant artificially created thoughts in a target's mind. The target can be misled.

One part of the project included the development of the "invisible assassin". An unsuspecting target could be made to harm others, which will cause the target to be arrested. The assassins would make their victim's death appear to be the result of natural cause. There would be no signs of external injury, chemicals in the body, or evidence of a struggle. The actual cause, "mind control."

In 1994, Ronald K. Siegel, an Associate Research Professor in the Department of Psychiatry and Biobehavioral Sciences at

UCLA wrote a collection of case histories on mind control. In 1998 a team of US scientist wired a computer to a cat's brain and created videos of what the cat was seeing. It is now possible, using supercomputers, to analyses human emotional EEG patterns and replicate them. These patterns can be stored as an "emotional signature cluster", and, at will, be silently induced to change the emotional state in human beings through resonating entrainment techniques.

## Synthetic Telepathy

"Synthetic telepathy" is a term used to describe the beaming of words, thoughts, or ideas into a person's mind by mechanical means, specifically an electromagnetic transmitter, similar to a radio or television broadcast, operating on the microwave frequency band. Animals are thought to have telepathic powers. Many biological effects observed in animals exposed to ELF fields appear to be associated with the nervous system. Human subjects exposed to 1310 Mhz and 2982 Mhz microwaves at average power densities of 0.4 to 2 mW/cm2 perceived auditory sensations described as buzzing, knocking, and rapping sounds.

Microwave pulses appear to couple to the central nervous system and produce stimulation similar to electric stimulation unrelated to heat. Electromagnetic radiation interferes with concentration on complex tasks. Microwave radiation can be used to induce headaches, fatigue, dizziness, irritability, agitation, tension, drowsiness, sleep-lessness, depression, anxiety, forget-fulness, and loss of concentration.

Microwaves can alter the permeability of the body's blood-brain barrier, which, in turn, can synergistically increase the effects of drugs. Using relatively low-level RFR, it is possible to sensitize large groups to extremely dispersed amounts of biological or chemical agents to which the un-irradiated population would be immune.

Sound can be transmitted even easier through the use of implants, such as cochlear implants. These implants can send electrical signals into the fluid of the inner ear, or implants that transmit sound vibrations via bone conduction. It is somewhat common for dental fillings to pick up audible radio waves.

Sounds and words, which appear to be originating intracranially, can be induced by signal modification at very low average power densities. The process called "Hippo-campal Neuron Patterning", grows live neurons on computer chips. Future battles could be waged with genetically altered organisms, such as rodents, whose minds are controlled by compute chips, engineered with living brain cells.

Atmospheric electricity can be used to suppress the mental activity of large groups of people. A sonic generator, turned to an infrasound frequency (below normal human hearing levels), can be used to create the feelings of depression, fear, panic, terror, and despair.

### Does watching TV affect Psi?

Every minute you are watching you are not practicing. This applies to psionics as well as baseball, running, mathematics, reading, or anything else. So how you are spending your time will influence the mastery of performance in any skill. It seems that most people would rather read about "it", watch "it", or categorize "it", because these skills are so much easier and more convenient than actual "doing it" skills!

## Teleportation

Psionics, the practice of extraordinary psychic power, is a mental function used by a person who uses the force of his or her mind to effect the environment and people around them. Many of these skills are used for everyday events, like knowing which lane will move faster, or shifting your position to avoid an accident, before any physical signs that an accident is about to occur. Psionics uses mental imagery and resonation to influence the physiological and psychological state of other people at a distant location, embodies the assumption that information can be transmitted, teleportated, from the consciousness of one person to the physical substrate of others, to induce these changes.

As psionic skills are mastered, influences may include moving people, in both action and thought, greater attunement to momentary and near future events, and enhanced communication skills. Through the use of psionics, a person can interact with the minds of others, influence events, without physically touching them, or travel across vast distances in an instant.

It seems that many people interested in psionic abilities wants to be able to use the most powerful abilities right away. Some evening they may decide they want to levitate or become invisible. After a few hours of "intense" effort results in failure, the task is abandoned, because it must be "impossible". The neophyte process is to see something on television (especially something enhanced by special effects), read a few articles or books, and try a few techniques in the evening when you are bored and don't feel like playing a video game, then complain that the psi energy is not working as seen on television.

Compare this concept to a more traditional physical skill, running. Perhaps you watch a running race on TV, like the Olympics, and decide that after 20 years of watching television and playing video games you want to become a world-class runner. You read some articles, learn some techniques, and buy special equipment to use during your practice sessions. As part of your self-analysis, you realize that you have had some experiences in running while growing up. You may have raced some neighborhood friends down the street, or even played organized sports where running was involved. You may know how to practice your proficient running skills. If really dedicated, practice will be the same time every day. After a few weeks of practice you discover that you can not run the Olympic qualifying standard, or even just a five minute mile. Then you discover that you are not seeing the same result as on television or on the video games. Playing the video game and seeing bright color graphics flash across the screen is more *awesome* than the subtle realities of applications often performed by a Master Psion.

There are so many people interested in learning about psionic abilities and wanting to go straight to advanced techniques. The subtle and more commonly used skills seem boring. The advanced skills, like teleportation or levitating a 2,000 object are more *awesome*, have more "oomph", and are the stuff of legendary psi skills. At the same time, the simpler, common skills are overlooked and not clearly understood.

## Chapter Seven

# CONDUCTIVITY OF THE MIND

We are all born with a receptive mind. Many influences in our society teach us not to open the receptivity of our mind. We are taught that following the norm is the correct way to live. Mental Health is the classic example. When anyone behaves outside of the central 70% or so of the "normal" population they must have a problem. They are, after all, abnormal by definition. So we are told that things like psionics, magic, ESP is only sought after by a few (abnormal; enlightened) people. Western religion has always been a primary deterrent to the open mind.

The mind of all beings and creatures exist in one of two states, and are referred to as either receptive or closed minded. People actually refer to a person as having an "open mind" or "closed minded". Only those things that enter through the normal senses (such as sight, sound, taste, touch, or smell) are considered by a closed minded person. The minds of all humans and animals are naturally receptive at birth. However, most human adult minds are closed, some are locked. A receptive person can voluntarily open his or her mind to friendly psionic contact, or it can be nudged open by psionic attacks.

Humans have been taught to neglect this natural ability. The "Age of Reason" was a highly influential era leading to psionic decline. The predominate thought at the time was to question everything, to believe only what you can see, touch, taste, smell, and feel directly. The extreme of this position is to arrest, torture, to burn at the stake, anyone with the slightest clairsentient ability. That this ability could have only been given by the Devil (negative energy) and not God (positive energy). That we are all created "in his image"... except for ESP, magic, creativity, humor, sarcasm, klutziness....! The open receptive mind of modern adult humans may not be part of the "new agenda".

Some psionic powers are only useful if the target mind does not know contact is taking place. Daydream, false sensory input, and invisibility are examples of powers that are only useful if the subject is unaware of the intrusion. Stealthy contact is the method by which Psions gain quiet entry into a mind. Line-of-sight is usually necessary for stealthy contact to take place.

Stealth contact requires the subject to be watched closely through the ethereal vision until an opportunity presents itself. If the attempt results in a miscalculation, detection is automatic. The targets mind has a good chance to locate the source of the attack. For a mind to be receptive, psionic defenses must be lowered, as in the case of a willing subject, a Psion, or a breached mind. A Psion's mind is always receptive.

## Properties of Energy & Matter

Contrary to popular belief, nothing is even remotely solid. At the sub atomic level it is well known that the nucleus radius to electron orbital ratio is one hundred thousandth. This ratio is approximately the same size as a spherical dot above the letter "i" (the proton) on the fifty-yard line in a football stadium (the orbital). Everything else is empty space. That's why neutrinos can zip right through anything completely unobstructed, and why the moon is only there when someone is looking at it. If we couldn't see vibrations of electron energy, the moon would completely disappear.

## Quantum Math

A basic principle in quantum math is that to understand a level of dimensions, we must go to a higher dimension. For example, a two dimensional plane is more easily seen when you elevate into the third dimension.

A three dimensional cube can be equated to three planar two dimensional sides of the cube, or the instantaneous change needed to increase the length, width, and height (volume) of the cube. This means that to increase three dimensional volume, simply increase one two-dimensional surface.

Taking this one step further, six one dimensional lines are needed for the instantaneous change needed to increase the length and width (two-dimensional area) of the three planes. Each of the three planes needs two lines (length and width) to increase its area. Three planes times two lines equal six lines total.

Continuing to look down in dimension, six points are the instantaneous change needed to increases six lines in length. The six points are "zero-dimensional". The equation $y(4) = 0$ is the instantaneous change needed to take the six points out of existence. However, mathematically, a problem occurs when we attempt to integrate something cube into the fourth dimension.

Remember, a cube isn't solid. Therefore, to attempt to visualize an integration of a solid is a misconception. The mysterious fourth dimensional shape is a tetrahedral axis shaped particle group of higher density. Any one-dimensional object is a line, a slice of a plane. Any two dimensional object is a plane, a slice of a cube. In reality, the lines of plane are not arranged parallel to each other. An infinite number of lines will be required to completely fill the plane. As our technology allows us to see in finer detail, we will continue to find more empty space in the plane that is capable of supporting an infinite number of lines.

Although the cube isn't solid, it must be made of something, some kind of particle. The particle must be capable of conveying information. At the simplest level, it may be to stay in the boundary, although it may also include information on electro-magnetic vibrations. Since there are different frequencies and/or strengths of vibrations with multiple simultaneous combinations, a zero-dimensional single point particle would be incapable of being the sole particle of a cube. A single point can spin, move, or remain at rest, but there is no chance of simultaneity or vibration.

The next possible alternative is the one-dimensional line or string. Any intrinsic universal characteristic will always be the simplest and at the same time most efficient option. On a musical instrument, the string of an instrument can convey a multitude of vibrations, tones, and harmonics. This means that there can be a lot of simultaneous information transmitted along a one dimensional string. There is no need to consider a particle made of two dimensional planes.

Reality, as we know it, appears to be existing on an infinite number of two-dimensional planes. We can move through every angle or vector direction. The way this actually works is by using axial directions as dimension. An actual working two-dimensional model of space would be an infinite array of two-dimensional axis shaped particles in a plane with the negative, or expansive force, vibrating through their matrix. In this model, light can travel in a straight line, or it can be warped or flexed, forcing curvature of light. If you took enough two-dimensional particles and curved and connected them into a spherical surface shape, it would be misinterpreted as three-dimensional. The actual two-dimensional electron is doing the same thing by orbiting spherically and mimicking a three-dimensional solid.

Now that we know that the basic workings of particles at the quantum level and we know vibrations occur in every possible direction, we find that a three dimensional particle will not sufficiently transmit vibrations along a diagonal. Therefore, a three-dimensional matrix is not totally efficient.

Particles capable of angular conveyance of information must be of a higher dimension and have the most efficient shape to pack space. This is a particle with ten-dimensions, or ten axis. In a ten-dimensional dodecahedral matrix, light is forced into zigzags. When a three-dimensional cube is integrated into the fourth dimension, the result isn't a snapshot of the cube in the fourth dimension, it is a tetrahedron with an increased density field matrix.

Remember, to have the most accurate view of a dimension, we must view it from at least one dimension higher. To view the tenth-dimension we need to see it from the eleventh-dimension.

**String Theory**

In the standard model of particle physics, particles (matter) are considered to be points moving through space, tracing out a line called the "World Line". To take into account the different interactions observed in nature, particles must include many degrees of freedom, such as position, velocity. mass, electric shape, color, spin, and so forth.

The standard model was designed within a framework known as Quantum Field Theory (QFT). QFT provides the tools to build theories consistent with quantum mechanics and the special theory of relativity. With these tools, theories can be built which describes three of the four known interactions in nature; electromagnetism, nuclear strong force, and weak nuclear force. However, gravity does not seem to fit into this model. For example, the force between two gravitons (the particles that mediate gravitational interactions), becomes infinite.

In String Theory, the myriad of particle types is replaced by a single fundamental building block, a "string". These strings can be closed like a loop, or open, with two ends. As the string moves through time it traces out a tube, or sheet, depending if it is closed or open. The string is free to vibrate, and the different vibrational modes of the string represent the different particle types, since different modes are seen as different masses or pins.

In super string theory, the subatomic particles we see in nature are nothing more than different resonances of the vibrations of superstrings, in the same way that different musical notes emanate from the different modes of vibration of a violin string. The forces between charged particles are the harmonies of the strings. The Universe is a symphony of vibrating strings. When strings move in ten-dimensional space-time, they warp the space-time surrounding them in precisely the way predicted by general relativity. Therefore, strings, simply and elegantly, unify the quantum theory of particles and general relativity.

Physicists theorize that during the "Big Bang" six of the ten dimensions curled up, or "compactified". Remember, for much of history, we were only familiar with three-dimensions. Only in recent history was the fourth-dimension opened. At the present, scientists are trying to complete identify and explore the fifth dimension.

## M-Theory

The name "M-theory was coined by Edward Witten of the Institute for Advanced Study at Princeton, New Jersey. It is unclear if the "M" stands for "membrane", "mystery", or "magic". M-theory predicts that strings co-exist with membranes of various dimensions. For example, a particle can be defined as a zero-brane (zero-dimensional object). A string is a one-brane, an ordinary membrane like a soap bubble is a two-brane, and so on. When three membranes vibrate, or pulsate, they create new resonance, or particles.

Quantum Theory shows us that our world, at a fundamental level, is not imaginable as mechanically the sum, or interaction of, truly isolated things. The mechanistic world-view assumes that bodies are isolable. Space would be infinitely measurable. Other characteristics would be unessential and the law of dynamic motion would be identical to causality. The mechanistically world view is not necessarily identical with the science of Newtonian Mechanics. Quantum; objects show that these assumptions fail. Objects have an inner structure, work permanently in interactions, are determined by more characteristics than space and impulse, and have statistical laws governed by both our past and our future, yet we only see part of the laws that govern.

Leaping to higher dimensions can simplify the laws of nature. The structures, which are observed by scientists in nature, are closely connected with the structures of the consciousness, with respect to thoughts, values, and emotions, The direct conscious influence onto these dimensional laws are of nature are what we know as psionics.

## Frame Dragging

Any object with mass warps the space-time around it, in the same way as a heavy object deforms a stretched elastic sheet. When an object spins, a distortion is introduced. The effect is called "frame dragging". Science has proven that the Earth's spin actually warps space and time around the planet. This is a modification to the simpler aspects of gravity set out by Newton.

Frame Dragging was predicted in 1918 by Austrian physicists Joseph Lense and Hans Thirring. In our movements, we create tiny layers of energy to swirl around our body in a minute space-time warp. By choosing to spin, or move, in a consistent direction, a particular kind of energy will be built up over time. This energy can be used in the development of psionics (karma).

Clockwise motions will lead to yang energy and counter-clockwise will lead to yin energy. Think of this energy in terms of electrical charge and current. Positive energy, by itself, has limited ability. Only with the interaction of positive and negative energy does real flow occur.

**Bina-mics**

There is an exchange of bits of info between the quantum world and the world humans can fully perceive. Everyday experiences lead us to believe that time flows in one direction, always forward. The second Law of Thermodynamics tells us that the tendency of the Universe is toward greater entropy, or disorder. This is why we never see a broken glass spontaneously reassemble its original, unbroken form.

The idea of *absolute time* and an *absolute now* is strictly a classical physics concept. However, when we examine how the future and past come together to create what we observe as the present, we begin to pull time in two directions. Natures' apparent direction of time is predetermined in many ways by quantum effects which appear as if it were composed of *absolute time* and *absolute nows*. This is an illusion of dual directions of time. From this perspective, real *absolute time* and *absolute now* are composed of the past and future and every *now* becomes a predetermining part of every *future now*, which in turn controls the *past now*. The only absolute is that everything about existence is interconnected. The real fabric of time and space is, in the end, determined by a fabric woven by every action that ever existed or ever will exist. The fabric is woven by connections. When "past space-time" combines with "future space-time" it produces "present space-time," or "potential space-time". KARMA!

## Wave Theory

Wave theory describes the behavior and properties of ordinary light, traveling forward through space at a speed of 299.79 million meters per second. It requires a positive time interval to travel a given distance. A common measurement is the "light-year."

However, there is a second solution of the wave equation. It is known as "the advanced solution". It describes a kind of light which also travels at 299.79 million meters per second, but which carries negative energy, and travels a given distance in negative time. When advanced-wave light travels from point A to point B it arrives at point B earlier than the time it left point A.

Creation becomes a loop in time. We observe the original starting point of the loop in time through each event that we witness at the quantum level as a repeated loop in time with a resulting phase difference at each event leading to motion through combined effect of space-time background.

## The Receptive Mind

A receptive mind is one that is open to psionic influences. A receptive mind is therefore also vulnerable to psionic influences. Therefore, the Psion will always have a defense operating at a low level of alertness, which can be immediately raised. Being on guard and vigilant is a good thing, being overly defensive can have a negative social impact. When a mind is forced open by psionic attack the target will experience trauma, it is stunned. This implies a change of brain chemical production and flow, which will lead to physical discomfort.

If a mind is receptive to psionic contact it can easily discontinue the contact. However, social courtesy is just as important as in real life. Closing the door on someone without any notice may lead to ill-relationships.

An overt psionic contact will cause many targets to immediately move their head to look toward the source of energy, or it may actually cause the target to stop moving. A Master Psion will often feel, and interpret, the psionic probe or attack without displaying any physical differences. Regardless of how stealthy a contact is made, contact is only temporary. After a time the receptive mind is aware of the intrusion and often who initiated the contact. Once a receptive mind is aware of the intrusion, the mind can be protected. The second reason is that the Psion will ultimately run out of energy and/or lose focus.

If the target is particularly busy at the time of the stealthy contact (engaged in work or play), contact can last twice as long before detection. If the mind is unconscious due to injury, or any other means that the mind is unable to detect the intrusion, it should be considered receptive.

Typically, eternal physical actions may cause the Psion to loose focus. A Master Psion will be able to quickly move in the most appropriate defensive mode. The receptive mind is always open for its own powers.

## Chapter Eight

# ETHEREAL VISION

The "ethereal vision", sometimes referred to as "mindscape" is the psionic environment, where explorations and battles occur. It can more accurately be described as ethereal vision with psionic senses. The Psion sees the physical world with external psionic senses. They see the ethereal vision by looking alternately inward and outward. Psions can see clearly into the ethereal vision. By concentrating on the mindscape, the Psion sees many images at once. All living plants and animals possess a psyche, or body, of psychic energy. From the ethereal vision an unshaped psyche looks like a glowing sphere of energy. It is this energy, which fuels a Psion's powers, attacks and defenses.

The ethereal vision is full of extra detail and impressions. The Psion's view will include all the minute features which the conscious brains of sentient beings have learned to dismiss. The Psion may note the unique bark pattern of an individual tree, the exact placement of stones on the ground, the distinct colors of foliage, and the background sounds of the environment.

A simple exercise for the conscious sentient mind is to stop, just stop. Sit down, allow relaxation to occur. Do not work at, or try to relax. Allow relaxation to have its' time. Using your eyes only, begin to notice as many different colors, hues, tones, as possible. Then close you eyes and listen. Listen for the background environmental sounds. How far away can you hear? Can you hear the clouds?

WARNING: Repeating this exercise will heighten your senses. The everyday world around you will become brighter and louder. You will become more sensitive to sound, light, and other senses. You will talk quieter and calmer, and listen to the television and music at lower volume levels.

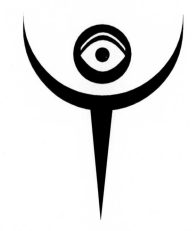

## Contact
A Psion may make contact with another mind for many purposes. A common neutral purpose is for communication and conversation. In relationships, Psions can easily determine if another person is lying, disguising an underlying topic, or determine if a mental illness is present.

## Long Distance Contact

One form of communication is to make long distance contact with receptive minds with which the Psion has previously had friendly contact. The initiating Psion activates the energy and focuses on the target. Long distance psionic contact generally does not have enough energy remaining to wage any sort of psychic attack. However, a Master Psion can influence behavior at any distance.

When using psychokinetic activity, there can be varying degrees of probability that the intended effect of a skill is a result from some other factor occurring at the time. Many times it is easier, and more efficient to influence the other factors affecting the target, i.e make something heavier, faster, or sharper. It is commonly rumored that when President Bush visited Japan, his vomiting experience was a result of psionic intention by a small Japanese martial art group.

It requires more sustained energy and is more difficult the farther away the target mind is. Concentration must be maintained for as long as it takes for the connection to get to the target mind. Knowledge of the terrain to be traveled toward the target is helpful. Being able to visualize turns and landmarks improves the efficiency of this skill. This is typically performed through seated or lying meditation, although I have known it to occur during active meditation in extreme circumstances.

## Line-of-sight

Many psionic powers require a line of sight, especially by neophyte Psion. The exceptions are generally found in the clairsentience discipline, and with friendly contact, some from the telepathy discipline.

A Psion can send out psi energy to locate a specific friendly, receptive mind. All psi energy are inherently identifiable and any psionicly receptive person will see the approaching psi energy, recognize who sent it, and decide whether or not to allow contact.

It is difficult to send psi energy to a long-distance mind if contact has never been granted before. It is difficult for the receiver to distinguish a specifically sent psi energy from a previously non-contacted source from those of random intrusion.

Psions have the ability to engage in long distant conversation, thereby making suggestions, posing questions, and explaining reasons. This process is generally not instantaneous as with normal sentient conversation. The energy can linger for a period of time. The receiving Psion must periodically check for these messages, as one would periodically check for their email messages.

## Psionic Powers

All psionic powers belong to one of five disciplines: *clairsentience, psychokinesis, psychometabolism, psycho-portation,* and *telepathy.*

### *Clairsentient*

Clairsentient energy perceives things beyond the natural range of the normal senses. "Clair" meaning "beyond", and "sentient" referring to a (Buddhist) concept, that humans are caught in the wheel of rebirth because they are attached to the physical world, thus being "sentient beings". Clairsentient talents are neither aggressive nor defensive, positive or negative. These talents are primarily used for intelligence gathering. Through this special increase of intelligence, the Psion will be able to improve their intelligence and wisdom. The negative aspect of clairsentient is susceptibility to illusions and hallucinations.

Prediction, another clairsentient skill, is a technique used in both magic and psionics. The theory is that time is an illusion and that we do not live in a linear world which unfolds sequentially. The theory holds that that the future exists in the same way that the past and the moment that is now exists. These time dimensions exist side by side. Occasionaly people go through the invisible barrier between this dimension that we call reality, and into another dimension such as the past or future. When this happens, the visions and experience gathered there form a glimpse of what is to be or what has been. The art of prediction is to slip into an altered state of mind that opens the door to these other dimensions. Psychics have a natural, or supernatural, ability to slip their consciousness into the next dimension and observing, in linear terms, the future.

Clairsentient skills include clairaudience, clairvoyance, detect, know alignment, know direction, know location, object reading, precognition, scrying and sensing.

## *Psychokinetic*

Psychokinetics is the movement of objects with mental energy. "Psycho" referring to the mind and mental powers; "kinetic energy" is energy that is in motion. Psychokinetic, at the core, is neither aggressive nor defensive, neither positive nor negative. However, a psychokinetic talent can lead directly to an aggressive or defensive condition. For example, producing heat is a common psychokinetic skill. The heat can produce warmth, be used to heal, or to cause injury. Influencing the movement of live entities, such as plants and animals, is much easier than inanimate objects. Further, it is easier to influence a non-living entity in motion rather than while it is at rest. The friction between stationary objects is difficult for many Psions to overcome. Psychokinetic skills mat not be very stealthy.

Psychokinetic skills include heat metal, influence object, levitation, magnetize, project force, push, remove curse, suppress magic, telekinesis and trip.

## *Psychometabolic*

Psychometobolic skills affect the physical body, usually by altering it in some way. "Metabolic" refers to the bodily rhythms of life, such as heart rate, temperature, and molecular structure. Sick tissue vibrates at a different rate than healthy tissue. Psychometobolic skills are generally used by the Psion on him/herself. These skills can also be used for both offensive and defensive purposes. The psychometobolic techniques are the ones most likely to cause direct and immediate physical harm, or relief of physical pain. Miscalculations in overestimating or under-estimating the strength of these techniques may cause the opposite result.

Psychometabolic skills include biofeedback, equilibrium, energy draining, enhanced strength, healing, mind-over-body, neutralize poison, resist cold and warmth.

## Psychoportive

Psychoportive applications alter and allow travel through multi-dimensional space. "Portive" means movement; or more precisely, moving around, as in porting a canoe around rapids. Occasionally, these skills are used for defensive purposes, i.e. to avoid a situation. However, most often, these skills are used for information gathering and research. It is important to understand and remember that transportation is a two way street. This concept has two aspects. First, when you "portage" in some manner, you have to be able to get back. Porting, then not being able to get all the way back will lead to psychosis. Second, is that when you place yourself on a "portive path", you are not alone. This is not an isolated exercise. Other entities travel these portive ways as well. Not only are you likely to experience unexpected encounters, but you must make sure your portive gateway is secured from intruders.

Psychoportive skills include astral projection, dream travel, spatial distortion, and time travel.

## Telepathic

Telepathy involves the direct contact of two or more minds or thoughts. Telepathy occurs all the time. It may be direct, or indirect. Business ideas often float around on the near ethereal plane. This explains why new business concepts are often "picked up" by many people within a small period of time.

Telepathy is primarily used for intelligence gathering. Knowing ahead of time what others are thinking will allow the Psion to gain wisdom and make better decisions. Be careful not to allow this skill to rage out of control. When you hear too many voices too often, you will not be able to hear your own thoughts. Telepathy is also used to influence the thoughts of others for the purpose of producing a personally desired result.

Skills include aura alteration, charm, dispelling, guarding, misdirection, persuasion, projection, psychic messenger, sending thoughts and suppressing fear.

## Chapter Nine

# PSYCHE ATTACKS AND DEFENSES

The previous five disciplines of psionic skills and talents deal primarily with the external, or physical dimensions of life. Psyche attacks and defenses are directed at the most inner human essence, the psyche, the soul. The psyche essence is about self-image, self-esteem, self-determined social order, self-confidence, self-determination, and self-survival. It is about "concept" rather than physics or physiology.

We are constantly positioning our self-concept with friends, family, acquaintances, and enemies. Psyche attacks and defenses are used every day, by every person having a relationship. Most often, the energy level is very low, in a range that is classified as socially acceptable. When the energy level raises, such as through anger, pain, or love, the level of psyche attacks and defenses are likely to raise. Look for the psyche offensive and defensive modes the next time you hear an argument. They appear as classic psychological conversational techniques used to either break an opponent down until they agree the way you do, or to be able to stay your course and be your own person.

**Psyche Defense**

Quite often the immediate initial raising of a psyche defense is enough to cause a psyche attack to stop. Psionics, like magic, is most effective when used in a stealthy manner. When used overtly, the Psion risks physical harm. The alternative choice would be to use psyche defenses. However, as noted in the energy use requirements of high-powered devices, during a psyche attack or defense the Psion will loose high-powered psi energy quickly. When this happens, physical energy is also drained.

Psyche defenses primarily protect against psyche attacks, but can be used to protect against some of the *telepathy and kinesthetic* techniques. The psyche defense response will automatically engage in a progression of psyche defensive strategies. The first psyche defense is often one of awareness, acknowledgment, or simple diversion. The Psion may further choose which psyche defense to use for an incoming psyche attack. Psyche defenses will automatically engage when a threat is perceived. Psyche defenses have no preparation time. They begin immediately. We all tend to be guarded with our inner psyche.

A Psion increases a psyche defense as soon as a psyche attack is perceived. There is no chance of failure that the psyche defense will be initiated. The variables which indicate the effectiveness of the psyche defense includes level of energy and appropriateness of psyche defense selection. Some psyche defenses are more effective against certain psyche attacks. The reverse is also true. The first psyche defense a Psion will use is known as the "primary defense". A Psion's primary defense automatically increases when an attack is perceived.

There are six psyche defenses, five common and one advanced. The five common are *intellectual fortress, mental barrier, mind blank, thought shield,* and *tower of iron will.* The sixth defense is only found with enlightened master Psions.

## Intellectual Fortress

This defense encases the mind in a powerful keep of mental energy to protect it from psyche attack. *Intellectual fortress* provides the best protection against *ego whip,* but it is extremely vulnerable to *psyche blast.*

## Mental Barrier

This defense builds a wall of guarded thought to protect against psyche attack. A mental barrier is extremely effective against a *psyche blast,* but vulnerable to a *psyche crush* attack. It is designed to sustain horizontal force, not vertical force.

## Mind Blank

This defense hides the mind from psyche attack, forming a vast featureless area, making it harder to target the closed mind. *Mind blank* protects best against *Id Insinuation,* while being vulnerable to *mind thrust.* Even in *mind blank,* there is a point of energy emanation. The Id is intentionally neutral. Thrusting may continue until the Id is found.

## Tough Shield

This defense forms a glowing shield to turn away a psyche attack. A *thought shield* defends most effectively against *psyche crush* but is vulnerable to *ego whip.* A shield is more flexible than a wall. Shields can be angled to deflect a horizontal or vertical attack. The weakness is that since the shield is smaller in size the edges are more easily breached. Therefore, a whipping action can go around the shield's edges and strike the target.

## Tower of Iron Will

This defense builds an unassailable haven for the mind. *Mind thrust* has a difficult time penetrating this defense, although *id insinuation* can breach its protection. When something is very large and strong, it is most easily destroyed by something small, from within. Something like rust, or the Id.

## Psyche Attacks

Psyche attacks require high energy. Psyche attacks are generally single directional and require line of sight. During a psyche attack, the aggressor will constantly move in an attempt to maintain, or improve, their position. However, a master Psion can bend, curve, or even bounce the line of attack. This makes finding the source of the attack more difficult.

Psyche battles may occur to manipulate minds so that other psionic powers can be used more effectively. Combat between Psions is overt and rare. It is often a momentous occasion, full of peril for both participants. If the battle is conducted in a public space the energy is so intense it will likely clear the area of all other animals.

Psions see into the ethereal vision and can sense the attacker's psi energy. A non-psionic person cannot see into the ethereal vision and often has a hard time conceiving of its existence or use. The attack will feel like a mental blow to the head. If the attack succeeds there will be an immediate and unshakeable presence in the mind, much more severe than the feeling of "someone's watching".

Experienced Psions will be able to immediately identify the type of defense the defender is employing. With this knowledge the Master Psions will always choose the form of attack the defender is most vulnerable to at the current time. As the defender chooses a more appropriate and efficient defense, the Master Psion recognizes this change and immediately alters the attack. Depending on the energy level of the Maser Psions, this exchange of energy, paree and thrust, can last for hours. When this intense psyche battle occurs, both parties will likely need extra sleep.

The Psion versus Psion battle then comes down to two factors. First, and most importantly, is the ability to recognize the type of psyche attack and psyche attack changes, and to be flexible enough to continually change to the most effective psyche defense. Second is the strength and endurance of Psion's energy. Typically these confrontations will use a lot of energy and cause fatigue. Endurance is very important to maintenance and survival of the Psion.

A Psion's mind is much more difficult to attack because the Psion will immediately increase their psyche defenses and send out psionic probes. If the target mind is already spending Psi energy or putting up a psyche defense, stealth contact will generally not be possible. A more typical approach would be for the attacking mind to initiate a subtler psionic power such as "trip".

Targets can attempt to locate the attacker by making intellegent checks. If the attacker is invisible or hidden in some other way, the non-psionic may have no idea who or where the attacker is. If the attacker is hidden in some way the defender may have to employ psionic means to locate them. An easy method to remain hidden is to attack from within a crowd. Non-psionic people will have problems in attempting to identify specific sources of energy in large groups.

The five psyche attack forms are *ego whip, id insinuation, mind thrust, psyche blast, and psyche crush.* Psions will use all five forms at varying degrees of effectiveness.

## Ego Whip

This attack is comprised of stinging, insulting and hurtful attack forms. In the ethereal vision the psi energy may be shaped as whips, scourges, flames, chains, filth; anything that assaults the targets self-esteem or individuality. *Ego Whip* works best against the *Mind Blank and Thought Shield* defenses. It can also be used as a defense to parry an incoming psionic attack.

The defender can become dazed, both emotionally and psychologically for a period of time. They will appear off balance regarding clear thought and action. Immediately after a successful attack the defender will be more vulnerable to suggestion, especially long term attitudes changes. The effect of a single ego attack is fleeting but repeated attacks can create a cumulative effect.

## Id Insinuation

This psyche attack manipulates the victim's subconscious, blurring the disciplined barrier between prime native needs and social constraints. The attack mode tends to use blurry, subtle psi energy that attempt to blend into the defender's construct like a chameleon. Id Insinuation works best against the *Tower of Iron Will* defense.

The *Tower of Iron Will* is effective against a significantly larger attacking force, yet is vulnerable to a small amount of psi energy. When *Id Insinuation* is successful, the victim is stunned and unable to act for a period of time. In a sense, the mind (the Tower) has been breached, causing a loss of energy. Thus, the lack of ability, or mental resources, to respond.

## Mind Thrust

All stabbing and piecing psi energies fall into this category. In the mindscape, this psi energy may appear as spears, arrows, darts, lances, needles, etc. A thrusting force attempts to suddenly pierce psyche defenses. Works best against the *Mind Blank.*

This technique is similar to the board game "Battleship". The attacking Psion randomly attacks and psychologically probes the psyche, until they get a hit (or push someone's buttons). Then they begin to attack in a near, unseen radius, to determine a pattern, a plane of vulnerability, until they eventually "Sink the Battleship". Some of the defenders psionic powers may be shorted out. When used on a non-receptive mind there is no effect.

## Psyche Crush

*Psyche crush* attempts to use an overwhelming, crushing force. An avalanche, hail storm or trash compactor are examples of *psyche crush*. The attack will feels as if it is coming from above. *Psyche crush* works best against *mental barrier* defense. Physical damage is likely to occur. This is a high-energy technique. This psyche attack will likely leave the attacker with some physical fatigue and the need for sleep or general rest.

## Psyche Blast

This technique functions like an explosion of destructive psionic force. Dynamite, an earthquake or a powerful missile are examples of ethereal vision versions of *psyche blast*. In psychological terms, this is similar to euphoric mania. It is typically the last and final attack used, for two reasons. It will have a highly negative impact on all creatures but those of the highest level Psion, and second, this takes all the remaining psi energy of the attacking Psion to perform, attacking and defending.

The attacker will have drained themselves of all remaining psi energy. Physically, this will nearly always cause the attacker to sleep shortly after the event. The defender will likely suffer long-term emotional psychological damage. If the defender has significantly lower energy and power levels, or is a non-Psion, psychologically damage can be permanent.

# CONCLUSION

What is it you are trying to learn about psionics? How do you spend your time practicing? If you spend you time categorizing, listing, and quantifying, you are likely to end up with some sort of compendium, an encyclopedia. A book that you can neatly place on your self, take off when you feel like it, and carry it around where ever you go. Or, you can be a "doer". The more you practice psionics the better able you will be able to perform psionics. The more consistent you practice specific skills the better you will be able to perform them. Chaotic training leads to chaotic results. The more you ask questions about psionics the better able you will become in asking questions about psionics. You will become what you do most.

The Universal Warrior should accumulate as many skills as possible, including philosophy, mathematics, science, fine arts, performing arts, martial arts, magic and psionic arts.

- To deny the truth without any grounds for doing so is to hold an unhealthy degree of skepticism.

- So, for better or worse, nearly every thing has an effect on your body.

- To improve the quality of your psionics, become a keen observer of life.

- There are more things in heaven, and earth, and the skies than we will ever imagine.

Just for today I will give thanks for many blessings.
Just for today I will not worry.
Just for today I will not be angry.
Just for today I will do my work honestly.
Just for today I will care for the earth.
Just for today I will be kind to my neighbor.
Just for today I will be kind to every living thing.

# GLOSSARY

**Asymmetric techniques** – exploration, discovery, resolution, and reinforcement of self-regulation processes which relate to specific manifestations of adoption.

**Awareness** – knowing that you know.

**Bio-energetic techniques** – act in relation to sets of general correspondences and regulatory functions which exist in the normal healthy body.

**Channeling** – the belief that spirits can speak through mediums or psychics.

**Chemical energy** – the result of a chemical reaction of some kind.

**Chi** – energy; In Chinese and Japanese (Mikkyo) Buddhism, *Chi* is based upon intention. The concept that *Chi* can be regulated in the body and moved by way of mind force. In Japan, the center of the Chi in the human body is called the *Hara*.

**Clairsentient** – energy that perceives things beyond the natural range of normal senses.

**Consciousness** – being awake; we are often aware of our sleeping dreams and/or not being aware while day-dreaming during waking hours.

**Devotion** – minor psionic powers.

**Diamagnetism** – the phenomenon exhibited by substances that are repelled by the poles of a magnet and thus lie across that magnet's line of influence, i.e. have a susceptibility to magnetism.

**Disciplines** – categories of psionic powers.

**Electrical energy** – the product of voltage times current.

**Elemental spirits** – fairies, gnomes, trolls, mermaids, etc.

**ESP** – extra-sensory perception; the term was first coined by Dr. J. B. Rhine (1896-1980).

**Ferromagnetism** – the phenomenon exhibited by substances such as iron that increases magnetization with applied magnetizing field and persists after the cessation of the applied field.

**Functional dynamics** – the principles that techniques built on the recognition of relationships, correspondences, actions and reactions.

**Ganzfeild experiment** – a procedure to increase psi abilities by eliminating one or more of the natural sense, such as sight and sound.

**Ghost** – the discarnate spirit of a physically dead person or animal.

**Heat energy** – natural chemical energy which produces the sensation of heat.

**Kundalini** – the Yin principle.

**Line of sight** – the visual eye contact of a target.

**Ley lines** – a theory that the world is criss-crossed with a series of invisible magnetic energy.

**Magic** – the use of spells, potions, and incantations to create an affect upon others or upon circumstances.

**Magician** – a person who practices magic.

**Magnetic domain** – one of the regions in a ferromagnetic solid in which all the magnetites have their magnetic moments aligned in the same direction.

**Mental defense** – the ability to identify, divert, or absorb psionic attacks.

**Nuclear energy** – the result of splitting or fusing atoms into lower energy states.

**Obstruction** – anything that hinders a person's normal vision blocks line of sight.

**Physiognomy** – the art of reading ones character by references to facial features.

**Paramagnetism** – a weak magnetic condition of substances that have a small positive susceptibility to magnetism.

**Physiology** – the chemical or internal make-up of a person, animal or object i.e. what makes us, us?

**Poltergeist** – a noisy, disgruntled ghost.

**Possession** – when an alien spirit enters a person's body and takes control of it.

**Potential energy** – stored energy.

**Prediction** – any of a variety of techniques used to determine future events.

**Primary defense** – This is the defense mode a Psion learns first.

**Psion** – a person who uses the force of his or her mind to effect the environment and inhabitants around him.

**Psionic activity** – making an attempt of psionic attack or initiating a power results in psionic activity.

**Psionic energy** – extension of the electric current running through it.

**Psionic strength** – the energy and focus level available for psionic use.

**Psionics** – the effecting of something at a distance through the electro-magnetic field using intention and often focusing tools (such as a line drawn or art template). The practice of extraordinary psychic power.

**Psychic** – from the root word Psyche, meaning "of the soul"; phenomena and individuals whose nature is beyond the current bounds of scientific explanation.

**Psychokinesis (PK)** – the movement of inanimate objects by persons using paranormal powers.

**Psychometry** – the principle that each and everything in the universe is vibrating and that within the molecules and matter of any given object their histories are recorded.

**Psychometabolic** – skills affecting the physical body, usually by altering it in some way.

**Psychoportive** – skills which alters and allows travel through multi-dimensional space.

**Psychotronics** – the interaction of mind and matter.

**Qi** – Chi; the energy within all living things, and is especially strong in humans.

**Sciences** – major powers of a given discipline.

**Soul** – the real you.

**Spirit** – an entity that is alive, living in the ethereal realm.

**Spirit Guide** – helpers, guardian angels.

**Synthetic telepathy** – a term used to describe the beaming of word, thoughts, or ideas into a person's mind by mechanical means, specifically an electromagnetic transmitter, similar to a radio or television broadcast, operating on the microwave frequency band.

**Skeptic** – those who refuse to believe in the phenomena of the paranormal.

**Telepathy** – the reception of knowledge without the use of the five common senses.

**Time** – $\dfrac{\text{energy x space}}{\text{oscillation}}$

**Trance State** – an altered state of consciousness that is between sleep and wakefulness.

**Touch** – a bio-generic technique.

**Voltage** – the mass volume of energy and current is the amount of flow of the energy.

# PSIONIC BELT REQUIREMENTS

| LEVEL | A1 | A2 | A3 | A4 | A5 | M1 | M2 | M3 | M4 | M5 | MP |
|---|---|---|---|---|---|---|---|---|---|---|---|
| **WISDOM** | | | | | | | | | | | |
| Yoga | 5 | 7 | 9 | 13 | 15 | 17 | 19 | 21 | 23 | 25 | 30 |
| **CONSTITUTION** | | | | | | | | | | | |
| Swim or Run (x 2) | .25 | .5 | .8 | 1 | 1.5 | 2 | | 2.5 | | | 3 |
| Fasting | 12 | 18 | 24 | 30 | 36 | 48 | | 60 | | | 72 |
| Stay Awake | 12 | 18 | 24 | 30 | 36 | 48 | | 60 | | | 72 |

**INTELLIGENCE**

| LEVEL/SKILLS | 1 | 2 | 3 | 4 | 5 |
|---|---|---|---|---|---|
| 1 | 23 | ~ | ~ | ~ | ~ |
| 2 | 39 | 3 | ~ | ~ | ~ |
| 3 | 51 | 11 | 1 | ~ | ~ |
| 4 | 59 | 17 | 3 | ~ | ~ |
| 5 | 67 | 23 | 11 | 1 | ~ |
| M1 | 71 | 29 | 17 | 3 | ~ |
| M2 | 73 | 37 | 23 | 5 | ~ |
| M3 | * | 41 | 29 | 7 | ~ |
| M4 | * | 51 | 37 | 11 | * |
| M5 | * | 59 | 41 | 13 | * |
| MP | * | 61 | 51 | 17 | * |

There are five kyu (beginner) levels and five dan (master) levels in the Psion's training. These levels reflect direct confirmation to the degree of self-contained enlightenment in psionics ability. The Psion's training is very tedious, demanding, and exhausting. Periods of downtime and rest are recommended and necessary for revitalization and recovery.

To achieve a level one (red) earth sash in Psionics, the practitioner has to learn the 5 Tibetans and do 5 repetitions as part of a daily or weekly routine or be able to hold an asana for at least 5 minutes, be able to swim .25 miles or run .5, fast for 12 hours, stay awake for 12 hours, and learn at least 23 level one skills.

For a level two (orange) water sash the practitioner should complete 7 reps of the 5 Tibetans as part of their daily or weekly training or be able to hold an asana for at least 7 minutes, being able to swim .5 miles or run 1, fast for 18 hours, stay awake for 18 hours, and know a total of 39 level one skills, and 3 level two skills.

A level three (yellow) fire sash requires doing 9 reps of the 5 Tibetans daily or weekly or be able to hold an asana for at least 9 minutes, being able to swim .8 miles or run 1.6, fast for 24 hours, stay awake for 24 hours, and learn 51 level one, 11 level two, and 1 level three skills.

A level four (green) wind sash requires 13 reps of the 5 Tibetans daily or weekly or be able to hold an asana for at least 13 minutes, being able to swim 1 mile or run 2, fast for 30 hours, stay awake for 30 hours, and know 59 level one, 17 level two, and 3 level three skills.

A level five (purple) sash requires 15 reps of the 5 Tibetans daily or weekly or be able to hold an asana for at least 15 minutes, being able to swim 1.5 miles or run 3, fasting for 36 hours, staying awake for 36 hours, and know a total of 67 level one, 23 level two, 11 level three, and 1 level four skills.

After these five sashes are earned, there are five more dan or master levels (sometimes called astral levels) which represent the higher degrees of the psionic arts. The eleventh, or last level, is awarded only to a Master Psion (MP).

Please e-mail us at the website www.hoshin.us or join our free Yahoogroups chat if you have any questions or wish to share your experiences.